WAR-TORN SKIES

OF

GREAT BRITAIN

HERTFORDSHIRE

Contents

First published 2007 by
Red Kite
PO Box 223,
Walton on Thames
Surrey, KT12 3YQ

www.redkitebooks.co.uk

Series editor
Simon W Parry

Design and layout by Steven J Postlethwaite
Printed in Malta by
Progress Press.

ISBN 978-0-9554735-1-7

Introduction

With the passing now of some sixty one years since the end of the Second World War, and rapidly heading towards the centenary for that of the First World War, it can be difficult to imagine some of the events that took place in the skies over Hertfordshire. The very people who took part, or were eyewitnesses, get fewer and fewer each year.

However, evidence related to this history is not always from such obvious sources; sometimes a little personal research can reveal fascinating details; that decaying bramble draped brickwork is possibly all that's left of an aerodrome bomb-dump, the delightful springtime blue-bell carpeted woodland that people enjoy walking through today may have looked considerably different 65 years ago when it was the scene of a bomber crash.

For example, when one visits Oakmere Park in Potters Bar, a delightful setting with its ornamental lakes, some ninety years ago it was covered by fifty tons of mangled metal, all that remained of a Zeppelin which crashed there. It is possible, as in many counties, to walk around unaware of such events and happenings as so few have attracted permanent memorials.

The aim of this work is to make the reader more aware of the area's history, to utilise some of the eye-witness accounts no longer available first hand, and perhaps even stimulate further research to be undertaken in the future. This can be immensely satisfying, as one never quite knows where such an undertaking may lead.

For fifteen years or more I had been told of a field where a bomber came down in World War Two and as the years passed I became more interested, interviewing local people who witnessed the crash. I was able to establish that it was an American aeroplane, a B-17, and that sadly all onboard had been killed.

Many years later I walked across the field picking up fragments and conserving them. One day an identity dog tag from one of the crew was located, since this bore details such as parents' address etc I wrote to all families with the same surname in that American town. Incredibly the first letter I received back was from the crew member's younger brother, to whom the dog tag was returned. We correspond quite regularly now; thirty years ago I could never have imagined that I would be in contact with relatives from one of the crew of 'My Bomber'.

Another important source of information has been the war-time schoolboy. Any self-respecting schoolboy could more often than not reach a crash site before the Home Guard and of course leg it away even faster if discovered, often with pockets bulging with aeroplane fragments. This was considered a serious crime at the time and could carry a fine of some severity if caught.

One young looter was to recount to me over half a century later that his self respect was slightly dented on one occasion. First to get to the crash of a B-17 he managed to take some items then, struggling to cycle away from two Home

Guard men, he was finally caught. He later admitted that his small bicycle was quite simply not able to gather the required get–away speed or maintain stability. This was due to being 'hindered by two browning 0.50 calibre machine guns across his handlebars and a long jangling belt of ammunition trailing behind him'. Many of these 'Liberated' fragments survive today, much to the delight and assistance of the modern researcher, although a few did not survive the clearing out by mothers when their sons were completing National Service in the 1950s.

Larger items such as a wing tip from the B-17 at Weston and a sizeable section of fuselage from the Kimpton Me110 sadly attracted the attentions of scrap merchants in the 1960s and 70s. Such items that have survived provide small tangible pieces of history which can illuminate any research work.

Further tangible evidence has been obtained from the many crash site excavations that have been conducted by dedicated aviation archaeologists and metal detectorists.

So in examining Hertfordshire's association with aviation we will see that the twenty five years between 1920 and 1945 is probably the peak period. However events that took place earlier, sometimes much earlier, all have a significant part to play in an analysis of the county's rich aviation heritage.

Outbuildings still remain at Hunsdon airfield hidden in nearby woodland.

THE HISTORY OF HERTFORDSHIRE'S INVOLVEMENT WITH FLIGHT BETWEEN THE YEARS 1784 -1945.

The county of Hertfordshire was to experience the first successful manned ascent by balloon in Britain. This was made by the Italian diplomat Vincenzo Lunardi, accompanied by his dog, cat and a caged pigeon, and it took place on September 15th 1784. This event formed what was also to be Hertfordshire's first association with aeronautical events. The ballooning pioneer and his trusted pets ascended from Moorfields in London, touched down in North Mimms (where he released the cat as it was rather agitated, the dog and pigeon carried on with him) and finally landed at Standon Green End at Thundridge near Ware. This second landing spot in a field called Long Mead later had a memorial constructed to the occasion, locally known as the Balloon Stone which still survives to this day. Therefore one might say Hertfordshire has had an association with the desire to become airborne for some 222 years.

Well over a century later it is notable that this area would have yet another aviation connection for South Mimms would become home to Sir Hugh Trenchard First Marshal and founder of the RAF. Evidence of his family's residing in the district is sadly indicated by the presence of a tiny grave in the Mutton Lane cemetery at Potters Bar, being that of his infant daughter.

The county has also been strongly linked with engine powered flight for the best part of a century, a connection not always one of success, achievement or technical development, for on many occasions it has involved bitter loss of life and downright tragedy.

In the autumn of 1912 a small flimsy aircraft fell from the county's skies to end up as a smashed tangled mass of splintered wood, wires and fabric deep in a thick hawthorn hedge just outside Graveley. For the locals and media this was quite a point of interest, aeroplanes were rare enough in those days, but to have one come down on your doorstep was major news. Tragedy was involved here for both the RFC crew were killed in the incident. Historically the crash is important as it is one of the first crashes involving a military aircraft on UK soil.

Moving on from the days of this shattered flimsy little craft, aviation incidents and happenings did not really come into play again until the First World War period. Aircraft passing overhead were then slightly more frequent but still very much a "George quick come outside and look at this" spectacle.

As World War One progressed not all things passing through the Hertfordshire skies would be welcome, even if still viewed with much interest. This was the era of the German Zeppelin, and for the first time in nearly a thousand years an invading enemy could regularly cause death and destruction to the population. The enemy could access and seemingly pass unhindered through the British skies. Surrounded by German propaganda the effectiveness combined with the sheer size of these airships was a cause of grave concern. This concern manifested itself in many forms, not least the numerous printed postcards of the time showing Zeppelins, their destruction, and a whole host of caricatures and cartoons with links to these airships....Britain was truly gripped.

Hertfordshire was once again at the forefront when the German Schutte Lanze SL11, captained by Hauptmann Wilhelm Schramm, was shot down at Cuffley by Lt W Leefe-Robinson amidst great cheers from the public. They would cheer even louder when a short time later one of the newer Zeppelins captained by the famous Leutnant Heinrich Mathy was shot down by 2nd Lieutenant W J Tempest and crashed in a ball of flame onto Oakmere Park at Potters Bar.

Both these victories were largely attributable to the use of the newly developed Brock-Pomeroy types of incendiary bullet. Advancing technology had saved the day; the threat from the Zeppelins was now all but over. In just under ten years the huge, ominous, threatening shapes of airships returned once again to the skies of Hertfordshire. On this occasion there was no military threat from an airborne enemy for these were the R100 and its sister ship the R101 based at Cardington. They heralded the development of peacetime airship passenger services, however several serious crashes combined with ongoing developments in aircraft meant that this method of transportation was ill-fated and by the mid 1930`s would be shelved.

One invention that increased confidence in the ability to survive such hazards was the parachute and in 1926 the first European branch of the Irvin Air Chute Co was established at Letchworth. By 1945 over 1500 parachutes were produced at the plant each week. This company had set up the Caterpillar Club in 1922 for all whose lives had been saved by the use of a parachute, membership involved being awarded a small gold caterpillar badge. By the end of World War Two the club would have over 34,000 members worldwide. The company is still there today, a landmark link to Britain's aviation history.

In 1934 Hertfordshire's main connection with aviation was at Hatfield with the de Havilland family, who moved their factory here from Stag Lane in Edgware. Production at Hatfield literally took off, producing a series of small commercial style models mainly for the wealthy, but with a vested interest from the military as well. Models that were produced at Hatfield in the 1930s included the Gypsy Moth, Tiger Moth and a whole host of other small to medium size aeroplanes.

During the 1920s and 30s many aerodromes were constructed or modified and enlarged to cope with the huge inter-war period development of sporting, passenger and postal services. On 31st May 1933 Amy Johnson the famous aviatrix and her husband Jim Mollison visited Hatfield in relation to their world record attempt in the de Havilland Rapide named Seafarer. In the 1930s de Havillands at Hatfield produced the Comet Racer, a twin–engined cantilever monoplane. One version, painted mainly bright red and named Grosvenor House, went on hold the world's attention in 1934 when it completed and won the Mac Robertson Air Race from London to Melbourne in Australia. Another significant site for the production of aircraft was at Radlett where Handley Page manufactured civil aircraft. During World War Two the site produced such famous bombers as the Hampden and Halifax.

Aircraft had become such a familiar sight now that school boys could collect cigarette cards illustrating the various types and many became highly proficient in spotting. However with the outbreak of war in 1939 the possibility that enemy aircraft would soon be overhead was once again real.

One method of protecting targets from this threat was the raising of single or numerous barrage balloons above them, but in the early stages of the war the only associated threat seemed to be the occasional balloon that broke free, like the one in 1940 that dragged its cable knocking off a few chimney pots in London Road Baldock, until coming to earth on Clothall Common.

Aircraft recognition was now of utmost importance and numerous spotter units were set up. Sometimes their operational base was a simple sand-bagged hole hidden in a hedgerow, uncomfortably crammed with Royal Observer Corps personnel. Other times they may have had the luxury of a small wooden hut, I remember one of these huts remaining until the 1960s when it still had tattered copies of the wartime aircraft recognition posters pasted to its slatted walls. From the spotting stations on high ground it was sometimes possible to see flashes of shell bursts high in the sky from enemy guns at Calais.

It was not until the summer of 1940 that German aircraft began to make a prominent appearance in the skies of Hertfordshire. Previously the occasional Dornier Do 17 or high flying Junkers Ju 86P had been spotted, but from August 1940 things really began to get interesting.

On 30th August 1940 the Luftwaffe made a series of raids, one of which penetrated far inland to bomb Vauxhall's at Luton and took the raiders right over a large section of Hertfordshire. On this date the public witnessed the first aerial combats to take place in their skies for 26 years, and delighted in the downed Messerschmitt Bf 110 that crashed at Kimpton. Another raid on the same day against Radlett aerodrome resulted in the loss to the Luftwaffe of a Heinkel He 111 that crashed and burned out on the aerodrome at Hunsdon, a place that would later in this war be famously connected with Turnbinlite Havocs and Mosquito operations.

After this the Luftwaffe daylight raids returned to the solitary intruder occasionally machine-gunning a street or causing catastrophic damage as in the incident where a single Junkers Ju 88 bombed de Havillands at Hatfield on 3rd October 1940. Small arms fire and airfield defences managed to severely cripple this Junkers Ju 88 and it struggled to fly away eastwards eventually crashing in flames a few miles away on East End Green Farm at Hertingfordbury. Unknown to the crew their bombs had killed many workers and severely damaged sections of the workshop involved with the development of a new aeroplane; the Mosquito. This solitary raid set back production of the Mosquito by several months.

Ironically the Junkers Ju 88 was to become the Luftwaffe's most versatile aircraft type, equivalent to the Mosquito's role with the RAF. Aircraft production was dispersed and sub-contracted all over the country, although often not too far away. The ESA factory at Stevenage manufactured the wooden wing structures for the Mosquito, as well as producing their famous desks and chairs for schools.

After this incident enemy activity over Hertfordshire was limited to the night-time with solitary aircraft, or long streams of well spaced out high flying raiders, intent on bombing midland towns such as Coventry and Birmingham passing. During one of these night raids, on 19th September 1940, a Heinkel He 111P was hit by AA defences over London, severely damaged it flew on to crash into the very soft and marshy margins of the River Stort at Thorley Wash. Remains of this Heinkel He 111 including a propeller blade could be seen still jutting out of the reed-beds until fairly recently.

On the 16th October 1940 an enemy raider, this time another Junkers Ju 88, exploded high in the night sky showering wreckage and debris including its crew over fields just outside Bishops Stortford.

Despite these set-backs for the enemy, single incidents of raiders dropping bombs all over the county were common; hardly a Hertfordshire town, village or rural farm escaped some sort of attention from parachute mines, oil bombs, high explosive and numerous incendiary devices. It must be remembered that during the war years a total of 258 people were killed by German offensive weapons dropped or landing upon Hertfordshire.

The decline in enemy aerial activity over Hertfordshire during this period heralded the arrival of the night time Blitz for London. Many people still remember the orange glow "like a never ending sunset in the South" as the Capital received the majority of attention from the Luftwaffe. It was not until 1941 that aerial combat would once again be a feature in the Hertfordshire skies.

On 20th January 1941 an unidentified German raider (claimed to be a Dornier Do 17) flew down the railway line from Cambridge firing at random, the waiting room at Baldock station received several bullet strikes. Local rumours persist that another enemy aircraft machine gunned Stevenage Old Town high street, although this is unconfirmed.

In the April of that year two German aeroplanes, a Heinkel He 111 and Junkers Ju 88, would be shot down within 24 hours and crash within a mile of each other near St Pauls Walden.

However not all Luftwaffe aircraft were bombers, several contained spies who parachuted into Britain. One of these, Karl Richard Richter, landed near to and was captured in Tyttenhager Park at London Colney, ominously near to Hatfield where the secret production of the Mosquito was well under way. Quite what his mission was has never been determined, but the unfortunate

Richter was hanged at Wandsworth Prison on the cold and grey morning of 10th December 1941.

In July 1941 the lives of the German air ace Heinz Volker and his crew came violently to an end over Ashwell. Volker's Junkers Ju 88 nightfighter was the last enemy aeroplane to crash onto Hertfordshire soil during World War Two.

Just a few miles away over the Hertfordshire / Cambridgeshire border on 16th February 1942 a disorientated Junkers Ju 88 accidentally landed on Steeple Morden aerodrome, realising their error the crew attempted to take off but were stopped by an Armadillo armoured car firing on them.

In 1942 the Luftwaffe launched a series of operations known as the Baedeker Raids against historical and coastal towns of significance, such as Norwich and Exeter. These raids were conducted mainly by Junkers Ju 88s and Dornier Do 217s and on several occasions single aircraft penetrated very deep into the UK.

The nearest enemy casualty for this period was a Dornier Do 217E-4 that was shot down by a Mosquito nightfighter and crashed at Wimpole, only a few miles from Royston.

The occasional large bomb or salvo dropped near isolated farmhouses etc seems to be Hertfordshire's only involvement with these operations. Spies and double agents were still being dropped over the UK, perhaps the most famous Hertfordshire case being that of Eddie Chapman. A professional safebreaker, he was in prison in the Channel Islands when the Germans arrived. They persuaded him to become an Abwehr agent and parachuted him into England on 20th Dec 1942 with a mission to blow up the Mosquito factory at Hatfield. He immediately notified MI5, who realised the potential of the situation and wrecked a disused section of the factory giving the appearance to Luftwaffe reconnaissance that the mission had been a success, enabling Chapman to return to Germany and continue as a double agent.

This county also possessed several satellite airfields, most simple grass strips with a few outhouses. Some of these like Panshanger were used as decoys with wooden and inflatable aircraft to attract enemy attention. Many flat level fields would also be utilised as temporary training areas to the delight of local schoolchildren who could often get their first close up experience of types such as the Tiger Moth.

Notable also was Hertfordshire's involvement with SOE operations, their Lysanders using many isolated flat fields as temporary airstrips, and staff being based in large houses around the villages of Hertfordshire such as Station XII at Aston House, other stations were the Frythe at Welwyn and at Bovingdon.

With the entry of America into the war Hertfordshire saw its fair share of new visitors when aerodromes were development at Bovingdon and Nuthampstead. For many villagers and townsfolk the appearance of The Yanks was a period about which they still talk with passion, "who could forget country lanes full of strangely sounding raucous chatter late at night as these lads came back from the pub to their new home". With the start of the American daylight operations

Hertfordshire skies became packed with all types of aircraft from the usual RAF types such as Spitfires, Mosquitos and Lancasters to their new colleagues the Mustang, Thunderbolt and B-17 Flying Fortress.

On 18th February 1944 nineteen Mosquitos from 21 Squadron took off from Hunsdon joining up with other Mosquitos from 464 and 487 Squadrons to participate in the Amiens raid, one of the most famous of all operations against Occupied Europe. This raid bombed the prison at Amiens where high level French resistance and other prisoners were being held. Mosquitos from 464 and 487 Squadrons successfully breached the walls of the prison and radioed the result to 21 Squadron who returned home without bombing.

Another notable but tragic incident involving Mosquitos took place in 1943 when John de Havilland's aircraft collided with another Mosquito whilst flying near St Albans, all four aircrew involved being killed.

These packed skies inevitably led to increased risk of accidents not just to aeroplanes and their crews but often to the public below. In early 1944 the Luftwaffe launched Operation Steinbock, also known as The Baby Blitz, in an attempt to retaliate for some of the now huge day and night-time raids conducted upon Germany by the USAAF and RAF. This new offensive brought the occasional Dornier Do 217K, Heinkel He 177, Junkers Ju 188 and Messerschmitt Me 410 types over Hertfordshire.

On 19th February 1944 several very fast raiders (possibly Ju 88s or Me 410s) dropped a scattering of incendiaries and a single 50kg high explosive bomb on the edge of Nuthampstead airfield.

A newer and initially much more serious risk to Hertfordshire's residents appeared in 1944 with the arrival of Hitler's much vaunted new V Weapons. Firstly Hertfordshire residents experienced the throbbing pulsing sound of the V-1 Doodlebug, hopefully passing overhead, this was soon followed by the huge explosions and rushing sound that heralded the arrival of the world's first ballistic missile the V-2.

Both types of V weapons fell and exploded in Hertfordshire, the results of which can still be seen today by the careful observer: a patch of different coloured soil when a field is ploughed, or a shallow crater evident in the light of a sunset. This new offensive lasted about a year and, despite its initial morale lowering, the damage in Hertfordshire was minimal when compared to other areas. Once again technological advances helped make part of this new threat obsolete with the development of Radar predicted gunnery and the proximity fuze.

Many V-1's were destroyed as they skipped over the coast, although most impacts in Hertfordshire were probably attributable to those launched aerially from modified Heinkel He 111s. Against the V-2 rocket there was no defence for once it had been launched it attained supersonic speed, and nothing could combat or detect them. In 1944 some families living around Ashwell used to go up to the surrounding hilltops on very clear evenings when they could clearly see the V-2 rockets being fired from Holland.

The crowded skies had been very hazardous and there were several incidents of aerial collisions over Hertfordshire. On 12th August 1944 a B-24 Liberator and a B-17 Flying Fortress collided over Loudwater; and just fourteen days later two B-17s collided over Weston Park. Many people watched and listened in awe as hundreds of American bombers would formate and stack up over Hertfordshire prior to raiding targets in Occupied Europe and the Reich. Many also witnessed the return of ragged formations, including aeroplanes with engines out, streaming smoke or with noticeable damage such as flak shredded stabilisers and wingtips missing.

With Victory in Europe achieved in May 1945 the skies once again calmed down. The Americans headed back home to be demobbed or posted to the Pacific Theatre gave away food rations and other supplies, including leather boots, caps, gloves and jackets to grateful villagers as they departed. What wasn't given away, including aeroplane parts, stores, crockery and cutlery, was sometimes bulldozed into specially dug pits and levelled over.

For a short time the skies may have seemed peaceful, but from late 1943 the countryside around Hatfield had echoed and reverberated to the shriek and how emanating from the test bed of a new type of engine. The DH 100 prototype Vampire jet made its first test flight from Hatfield on 29th September 1943.

For Hertfordshire, indeed Britain and shortly the rest of the world, the dawn of the jet age had broken.

Hertfordshire Airfields

BOVINGDON

This airfield was constructed late in 1941 and completed in early 1942. On 15 June 1942, 7 Group, Bomber Command took up residence here. In April 1943 it was transferred to the USAAF Command as an operational B-17 base, later becoming home to the 92nd Bombardment Group (Heavy) 'Fames Favored Few' comprising of the 325th, 326th 327th and 407th Bomb Squadrons. This group was here from August 1942 until January 1943 and flew several operational missions from in September and October 1942. Then it was assigned to the 92nd BG B-17 Combat Crew Replacement Unit (CCRU) the 11th CCRU was also based here. Bovingdon was also the 8th USAAF Head Quarters and for a while General Eisenhower's personal B-17 was housed at this base. During the war years many famous film stars such as Clarke Gable, James Stewart and William Holden were assigned to the base.

Units to have operated from Bovingdon were:- 326th Bomber Squadron, 377th Bomber Squadron, B-17 CCRU and 11th CCRU. 92nd BG (Heavy).

After September 1944 Bovingdon became the European Air Transport Service Terminal, with thousands of American servicemen returning to the States from here. Three epic war movies were filmed here 'The War Lover' in 1961, '633 Squadron' and 'Mosquito Squadron' in 1964. Flying ceased in 1969 and the site was sold in 1976.

B-17E *Yankee Doodle,* **served with the 92nd Bomb Group.**

14

Today a prison 'The Mount' occupies some of the site, being built on the old technical and hangar areas. Some of the site is used as landfill and the crumbling runway surfaces now host a Sunday market. The only screeching of rubber to be heard now comes tyres of banger racing cars rather than B-17s.

BROXBOURNE

Originally the home of both the London Transport Flying Club and the Herts & Essex Aero Club that shared the facilities. During the war years Herts & Essex Aero Club became Herts & Essex Aviation, still based at Broxbourne where it remained after the war in a civil capacity. The airfield stayed in use until 1953. Today the site has been totally changed due to aggregate extraction and is now a gravel pit.

ELSTREE

Originally started out as a small grass airfield with a tiny hangar for the use of wealthy Polo players who utilised the country club at the adjacent Aldenham House in the 1920s and 30s. During World War Two the concrete runway was laid.

In 1941 Elstree became a Link Trainer School, large numbers of students now required training on individual and the team skills involved in flying the wide variety of military aircraft and the Links company had designed a flight simulator that could provide a certain level of training. The airfield was also used by Fairchild Aviation for aircraft modifications which included Westland Lysander IIIs and Wellingtons. Today it is still an operational civil airfield surrounded by many small industrial units.

HATFIELD

Home of the de Havilland Aircraft Company Ltd since 1934. Units based there:- RAF No 1 Elementary Flying Training School, No 5 Ferry Pool ATA, 2 (ACO) Sqn, RAF No 1 Anti-Aircraft Calibration Flight, then 116 Sqn. Closed in 1994. For further information please see sections Hatfield and the de Havilland Family and also Hertfordshire's Wooden Wonder or Timber Terror - the development of the Mosquito.

HUNSDON

Hunsdon was built by several agencies and contractors. Perimeter tracks and runways were laid by George Wimpey & Co Ltd, whilst the buildings were chiefly constructed by H J Janes of Luton. Work in earnest started on 9th October 1940 and the airfield was officially opened on 4th May 1941. It had initially

been planned as a satellite airfield for North Weald. Hunsdon was home to 85 Squadron and its Hurricanes, eventually these were changed for Boulton Paul Defiants, which in turn were changed for twin engine Douglas Havocs. Finally 85 Squadron operated Mosquitos before it transferred to West Malling in Kent.

The site at Hunsdon was made up of nine separate sites with living/technical quarters and even a cinema, totalling 448 separate buildings. Most of these buildings were Maycrete, Thornycroft or Nissen huttage. In addition to these were 16 blister type hangars and one large Bellman Hangar on the north side.

Squadron Leader V J Wheeler MC DFC of No.85 Squadron (right) in conversation with Wing Commander Harvey, CO of Hunsdon.

Units known to have operated from Hunsdon are:-
85 Sqn (Hurricane, Boulton-Paul Defiant, Havoc and Mosquito).
287 Sqn (Boulton-Paul Defiant II).
1451 Flight (Turbinlite Flight) (Boston / Havoc).
29 Sqn (Mosquito).
3 Sqn (Mosquito).
1530 Flight (Airspeed Oxford).
157 Sqn (Mosquito).
515 Sqn (Beaufighter, Boulton-Paul Defiant).
406 (RCAF) Sqn (Mosquito).
409 (RCAF) Sqn (Mosquito).

16

410 (Cougar) Sqn (RCAF) (Mosquito).

418 (RCAF) Sqn (Mosquito).

21 (City of Norwich) Sqn,

464 (Australia) and 487 (New Zealand) Squadrons (Mosquito)

264 Sqn (Mosquito).

488 (New Zealand) Sqn (Mosquito).

151 Sqn (Mosquito).

501 (County of Gloucester) Sqn (Hawker Tempests).

530 Sqn (Turnbinlite formed from 1451 Flight) (Boston / Havocs)

611 Sqn (Mustang IV)

154 Sqn (Mustang IV and Spitfire Mk6) forming Hunsdon Wing 442 (RCAF) using the now disbanded 154 Sqn aircraft.

The Airfield closed in 1947. Today little remains apart from the perimeter track sections, some small buildings in adjacent woodland and the seemingly defiant and indestructible Pill boxes.

Today a small Microlight club operates from the airfield, continuing Hunsdon's firm association with flight. In August 2006 Hunsdon's World War Two heritage re-appeared in the form of an unexploded hand grenade and 300 rounds of 0.303 and 20mm cannon ammunition spotted lying in a ploughed field. The Explosive Ordnance Disposal unit based at RAF Northolt carried out two controlled explosions destroying this potentially lethal legacy.

Some of the outbuildings remaining at Hunsdon airfield.

HUNSDON`S MOSQUITOS SENT TO PRISON:- THE AMIENS RAID

On 18 February 1944 a total of nineteen Mosquito FB.VIs took of from Hunsdon airfield on one of the most daring, skilfully planned and prepared for raids of World War Two. Eighteen of these aircraft were scheduled to attack Amiens prison, whilst one from the Photo Reconnaissance Unit (PRU) would record the raid and its effects.

For some while now members of the French Resistance had been held in this prison, individuals who would be vital in establishing secure networks and support once the Allied invasion had started. Several had already been executed and it was believed that a large number of the remainder were to be shot on 19 February.

It was considered imperative to make some attempt to breach the prison walls and hopefully give the opportunity for as many to escape as possible. The attack had to destroy the guard's hall and breach the walls to maximise the chances of escape into the surrounding countryside. The task of planning this raid was given to AVM Basil Embry who decided that No. 140 Wing based at Hunsdon would undertake this precision raid. No. 140 Wing consisted of Nos. 464 (RAAF), 487 (RNZAF) and 21(RAF) Squadrons.

The Wing Leader at this time was Group Captain Percy Pickard who, because of his inexperience in low level raids, undertook a ten hour conversion training course at Hatfield.

In support of the Mosquitos would be Typhoons of No. 198 Squadron. Each squadron was given a specific task: No. 464 was to place its bombs against the main prison walls, No. 487 was to bomb the guard's mess and make two breaches in the outer walls. If no prisoners could be seen escaping No. 21 Squadron was given the awful alternative, to bomb the prison itself.

A date for the raid still had to be picked, inclement weather had not improved by 14 February and time was running out. At 08.00 hours on 18 February the operational crews were briefed, a model was unveiled in front of them, and for the very first time it became clear just where they were heading.

A powerful memorial on the site of Hunsdon airfield. Such memorials are often financed by donation and erected by enthusiasts to ensure that events and people will never be forgotten.

The Mosquitos eventually took off into the snow swirling grey skies over Hunsdon and quickly faded from sight. The weather continued to deteriorate resulting in four crews losing contact with the formation and having to find their way home. Yet another set-back resulted from one aircraft developing engine trouble and also having to turn around.

Outside the prison in anticipation of the hoped for raid several resistance workers were walking past to assist with the escape. At one minute past noon the sound of Merlin engines was heard, increasing until three low flying aircraft could be seen bursting through the gloom. Within thirteen seconds a series of huge blasts occurred, vivid orange coloured flashes sending up huge fountains of shattered bricks. A direct hit on the guardhouse was also achieved. The mission had been a success.

Suddenly Pickard's aircraft came under attack from an FW 190 piloted by Feldwebel Wilhelm Mayer of 7/JG26. Machine gun and cannon fire splintered the rear fuselage and caused the tail unit to fall away. Unable to control the aircraft it crashed into a field at St Gratien, scattering debris across a wide area of countryside. Percy Pickard and his navigator Alan Broadley were killed instantly. A local girl ran to the scene and cut Pickard's medal ribbons and wings from his tunic, posting them to his widow shortly after the war. As he turned for home a Mosquito was hit by light flak and made a high speed crash landing in open country. The navigator was dead, the pilot survived to be made a prisoner of war.

In total 255 prisoners escaped, but in April some 260 survivors and those who had assisted in the escape were executed and buried in a defence ditch at Arras.

The cost of this raid was very high in terms of human life, but it proved that such attacks were possible. The importance of its effect on the morale for both the Allies and the French Resistance can never be underestimated.

A dramatic photo taken by one of the Mosquitos during the Amiens Raid.

HUNSDON'S TURBINLITES
The Havocs / Bostons and Mosquitos

Turbinlite was the name given normally to a converted Douglas Havoc Mk.I that was modified to carry a 2,700 Million Candlepower (2.7Gcd) Helmore / GC searchlight. This apparatus had been the brain child of Wing Commander W Helmore, and was constructed by the General Electric Company. The searchlight was housed in the nose of the aeroplane, along with AI Radar, and additional equipment in the bomb bay area meant that the aeroplane had no armament.

A total of 31 Turbinlite conversions were completed on Havocs/Bostons. The basic idea was that the 'Turbinlite' would fly paired with a 'parasite' Hurricane fighter. The Turbinlite aircraft would track down an enemy aeroplane with its radar, get to within 3,000 feet and illuminate the target allowing the Hurricane to intercept and hopefully destroy it.

Havocs fitted with the Turnbinlite searchlight were initially operated by 1422 Flight (Air Target Illumination Unit) which was formed at Heston in 1941. Then aircraft were operated by Nos. 1451 to 1460 Flights, later redesignated Nos. 530 to 539 Squadrons.

During the Luftwaffe's so called 'Baedeker Raids' in 1942 two Turbinlite sorties were flown from Tangmere in defence of Bath, involving Bostons from 1458 Flight and Hurricanes from 245 Squadron, both sorties failed to make contact with the intruders being sought.

The Turbinlite more often than not provided enemy defensive gunners with a bright target to aim at. Furthermore the carefully built up night vision of the Hurricane pilot was lost and should the enemy take evasive action pursuit was impossible.

Despite its innovativeness and logic this system of interception was finally deemed totally ineffective. In January 1943 Hunsdon's association with the Turbinlite was wound up, from now it was considered far more practical to allow the newly radar equipped Mosquitos to track down enemy intruders on their own.

The 2,700 Million Candlepower searchlight installed in the nose of a Havoc.

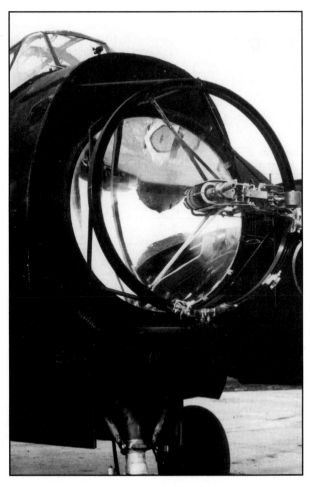

LEAVESDEN

Requisitioned in 1940 by The Ministry of Supply from Watford Corporation. Two large aircraft manufacturing plants (London Aircraft Production and Second Aircraft Production) were there building Halifaxes. A short while later de Havillands were also based there, the site being a satellite production centre to Hatfield for the Mosquito. The first Leavesden manufactured Mosquito was delivered in May 1942. The Leavesden site went on to complete and deliver a total of 1,390 Mosquitos. The airfield was equipped with a grass airstrip and remained open until 1994.

NUTHAMPSTEAD

Station 131 built by the 814th and 830th Engineer Battalions. Nuthampstead had the distinction of being the only purpose built USAAF airbase in Hertfordshire; it was also the highest at 460 feet above sea level.

Main units based here were:- the 55th Fighter Group (38, 338, 343 Fighter Squadrons) (P38 Lightnings) 398th Bomb Group (600, 601, 602, 603 BS).

On occasion the 20th Fighter Group flew from here in support of the 55th FG. The 55th FG became the first American fighter group to penetrate the skies over Berlin; this wartime milestone took place on 3rd March 1944. On 10th April 1944 the 55th introduced a new variant of the Lightning with a Plexiglas nose and room for a prone bombardier: this type became known as "Droop Snoot".

A decaying outbuilding at Nuthampstead. 60 years of erosion has taken its toll on the brickwork.

During the war there were two Luftwaffe attacks on the airfield and a V2 rocket later came down near the bomb dump.

On 2nd October 1944 Glen Miller and his famous orchestra gave a concert inside one of the T2 hangars. The airfield was equipped with three runways two T2 Hangars and fifty dispersal loops.

Nuthampstead's operational history closed almost as fast as it had sprung up, by 29th December 1945 there were no units listed there. Eventually it was handed over to the RAF who departed from all involvement here on 1st March 1959.

In the 1990s several outbuildings were demolished. In adjacent woodland small Nissen huts and crumbling brick revetments exist which were once part of the bomb dump complex. Surrounded by business premises and houses the bramble infested remains of at least one large outbuilding can still be seen.

Today a small grass strip is in operation for pleasure, agricultural and small commercial aircraft.

Two memorials exist outside the Woodman Public House to the 55th FG and 398th BG. The Woodman is in itself a shrine to those concerned with operations from Station 131 and houses numerous wartime artefacts and related exhibits.

The author would like to draw attention to the local research work of historian Russ Abbey of Nuthampstead Airfield Research Society (NARS) and that of Malcolm Osborne who supplied both information and illustrations for this publication.

One of the two memorials outside The Woodman Inn at Nuthampstead.

NUTHAMPSTEAD UNDER ATTACK!!!

During World War Two several of Hertfordshire's aerodromes attracted attention from Junkers 88c Nightfighters of the Luftwaffe unit NJG2. These early attacks were no more than brief bursts of gunfire and the odd SC50 bomb being dropped, sometimes the intruders would claim a Wellington bomber as a victory. Indeed just over the county border in Cambridgshire around the airbase of Bassingbourn several Wellingtons were destroyed in this manner. By late 1941 the intruder raids had ceased, but there was one event later on in the war that merits attention, this concerned Nuthampstead airfield in 1944.

On Sunday 14th May 1944 at 02.30 hours several crew of the 478th Sub Depot were conducting maintenance on a 398th Bomb Group B-17. Bob Robertson and Joe Spechulli were using a small light to oversee their work, and believe this is what may have got them noticed. They were still cautious as just 12 weeks before several fast enemy raiders had dropped a scattering of bombs over the airfield.

Just then a single engined fighter (positively identified by both men as a Focke Wulf 190) came hurtling over the airfield at low level with guns blazing, strafing the men working on the line. Fortunately no one was injured and just a few holes were put into the B17 being overhauled.

For a single engine German fighter to appear this far inland was putting

The 398th Bomb Group memorial at Nuthampstead.

Inside The Woodman Inn is a fantastic collection of artefacts.

some stress on its operational range. Even more mysterious is that several days previously the infamous Lord Haw Haw had welcomed the 'Triangle W' to Nuthampstead on a radio broadcast, promising that the Luftwaffe would soon be paying them a visit. Was this pure coincidence or had the Luftwaffe tasked a single aeroplane to undertake this 'welcome' mission?

The event was recorded by the 478th diarist, and has eyewitnesses to its happening, so there is no dispute as to its authenticity. The few FW 190 and Me 109 raids at this stage were restricted to Southern England's coastal regions, so this incident is all the more exceptional. Whether its pilot had been briefed to make this hazardous solo mission or whether something clandestine going on we shall perhaps never discover.

PANSHANGER

This small airfield began development early in World War Two as a decoy, to divert attention away from nearby Hatfield. It consisted of dummy aircraft, cars and even smoking chimneys, in fact it was so successful that many RAF pilots actually landed there.

The RAF No 1 Elementary Flight Training school set up there after a year or so and eventually the decoy buildings were all replaced with more permanent fixtures. In 1953 the RAF withdrew and Panshanger became a civilian airfield which is still operating today.

RADLETT

First opened as a grass aerodrome in 1929. In 1930 Handley-Page were based here producing civilian models, indeed they were the first UK company to be registered for aircraft manufacturing. Previously from the Handley Page manufacturing site at Cricklewood the company had produced a series of large bombers during World War One. These included the 0/100, 0/400 and finally the 0/1500 aircraft. The idea behind them being that they would have a range to bomb Berlin in revenge for the Zeppelin attacks on London.

The site at Radlett produced the Hampden and Halifax throughout the war years and carried on aircraft production in the post war period. In 1962 Sir Frederick Handley-Page died and by 1969 the company, with no viable future, went bankrupt. The airfield was closed in 1970 and has been subjected to extensive gravel extraction. One Hangar remains and is used for warehousing.

SAWBRIDGEWORTH

Upgraded from an Advanced Landing Ground in 1942 with much of this work being undertaken by W C French & Co. A T2 Hangar was erected along with 16 Blister type hangars, in addition to this were several 'Blenheim' Type aircraft pens. The runways were made of Sommerfield tracking. There was an experiment to use Coir matting (coconut husk woven into matting) in some areas, however this soaked up the moisture to such a degree that later on the Mosquitos of 'B' Flight No.4 Squadron were forced to transfer to Hunsdon whilst the matting was removed. Initially occupied by 2 Sqn (AC) RAF using Lysanders, Tomahawks and then Mustangs, this was an Army Co-operation squadron used for photographic work, artillery spotting and some leaflet drops.

Units known to have operated from Sawbridgeworth are:-
No.2 (AC) Squadron (Lysanders, Tomahawk 1 and Mustang)
No`s 63, 168 and 170 Squadrons (Mustang 1).
4 Sqn (Mustang then later in 1944 Spitfire (PR)
4 Sqn 'B' Flight (Mosquito PR16).
80 Sqn (Spitfire Mk.IXb).
182 Sqn (Typhoon 1b).
268 Sqn (Tomahawk Mk1 and 2, Lysander and Spitfire).
126 Sqn (Spitfire Mk.1X).
1419 Flight later to become 138 (SD) Squadron (Lysanders).
Special Duties and SOE used this airfield mainly for training, however there were also several operational agent dropping sorties conducted from here.

The airfield was closed in March 1947. In one of the blister hangars that was still surviving in the late 1960s the notorious Police killer Harry Roberts was finally caught after being on the run for weeks.

Today the airfield has faired better than Hunsdon. Large sections of perimeter tracking survive; particularly good areas are in Mathams wood. Here there are also two 'Blenheim' type dispersal pens complete with blast walls and an adjacent air raid shelter. Many of the runway sites are now in agricultural use. The old guardhouse, defence shelters and ancillary buildings are in quite good condition at Shingle Farm. Blounts Farm has the remains of one of the 24,000 gallon aviation fuel stores nearby. The cinema and entertainment centre was pulled down after the war to be re-erected in Sawbridgeworth town and is still in use today as a civic centre.

Note:- of the above airfields it is known from captured documents and photographs after the war that Luftwaffe reconnaissance flights definitely photographed Elstree, Hatfield, Radlett and Broxbourne on several occasions, and probably some if not all the remainder for which evidence no longer exists.

DECOY SITES / DISGUISES: - AN ATTEMPT TO CONFUSE THE ENEMY BOMBER CREWS

Initially two types of decoy sites were developed to confuse enemy bomber crews, known as 'K' and 'Q' sites. 'K' sites were for daylight use and 'Q' sites for night time use, not always separate sites as one could function in both roles. Obviously a fake airfield required dummy aircraft to add realism and a number of companies were approached to undertake their construction, including British Acoustic Films Limited of Shepherds Bush. The number of decoy sites increased in England and by the close of 1941 they had been attacked a total of 717 times. Further developments and requirements led to the establishing of night time 'QF' and 'QL' sites. These simulated factory environments using lights or fires to give the appearance of a target under attack.

At Panshanger not only was there a decoy airfield, but also dummy factory buildings. The entire site helped to distract attention from nearby Hatfield. Although Hatfield itself was disguised, large open runways stood out rather from the surrounding field pattern. To counteract these features, fake hedgerows and trees were painted on the surfaces with tar, cleverly aligning themselves with the surrounding genuine hedges. The continued success of these decoy sites led to the creation of much larger 'Special Fires' or 'Starfish' sites. These were positioned in the vicinity of towns or other strategic sites and ignited when the real target was under attack.

Hertfordshire had several varieties of decoy sites. At Puckeridge there was an example of the 'Q' site, whilst there was a 'K' site at Hoddesdon and a 'QL' site at Hatfield. Knebworth and Redbourn areas were the only two in Hertfordshire to have the much larger 'Starfish' sites, whilst there was a 'Q' site further east at Royston.

With the easing of Luftwaffe operations after the Baedekker raids of 1942 the need for the sites was considerably reduced. In 1942 the 'K' sites were finally closed down, and by 1943 all the 'Starfish' and 'Q' sites had been shut down, their jobs performed admirably. Countless lives had been saved and important industrial targets had reduced damage inflicted as a result of these decoys.

The newly erected memorial at the site of Sawbridgeworth airfield.

Hatfield and the de Havilland family

The de Havilland Aircraft Company Ltd was formed on 25th September 1920 by Geoffrey de Havilland. Up until this time the company's main aircraft production plant was based at Stag Lane in Edgware. By 1934 this had been relocated to Hatfield and so began a long legacy of aircraft development.

Born in 1882 Geoffrey de Havilland had a long association with aviation manufacture, having built two aircraft back in 1909 and 1910 shortly before joining the HM Balloon Factory. During World War One he worked for the Airco company. Once the war was over factories had manufacturing capacity that was no longer required and, like many similar factories, Airco's profits plunged; until Geoffrey de Havilland purchased it.

At this stage one of his best known designs was the DH-4 light bomber, which saw worldwide service and was particularly famous as the mainstay of the developing US Airmail system. In 1929 Sir Francis Chichester flew a de Havilland Gypsy Moth from England to Australia, continuing a long line of de Havilland aviation accolades.

Developments at Hatfield progressed through the 1930s with light, gracious and well constructed models. One of the most famous types was the DH-82a Tiger Moth, which went on to become a very versatile trainer in World War Two.

When production of this model ceased in 1945 over 8,811 had been produced. The fact that Geoffrey de Havilland was a keen entomologist is reflected in the names given to many of his aircraft models such as Puss Moth, Hawk Moth and Dragonfly.

However it is for the design and development of the Mosquito during World War Two that the name de Havilland will forever be inextricably linked. The first prototype Mosquito, W4050, flew from Hatfield on 25 November 1940 just ten months and twenty six days after its initial design. The second prototype, W4052, took off from Salisbury Hall, precariously utilising an adjacent ploughed field as part of its runway.

The Mosquito went on to become one of the most versatile aircraft ever produced. Sadly two of Geoffrey de Havilland's sons John and Geoffrey would die as test pilots, John whilst flying a Mosquito in 1943 and Geoffrey whilst piloting the DH-108 Swallow in 1946. Both are now buried in Tewin graveyard.

Initially it had been uncertain as to whether his enthusiasm for flying would ever have been passed on to his sons; Sir Geoffrey was to recall, "I first took my elder sons flying when they were five and three. One merely wished to know which way his spit would blow, and the other, mad about trains, asked to follow the railway lines.

For his unequalled services to aviation Geoffrey de Havilland was knighted in 1944. He went on to manage the company until his death in 1965, whereupon it became a division of Hawker Siddeley. During his lifetime he had designed over fifty types of aeroplanes, many examples of these can still be seen performing at air shows or are the coveted possessions of private collectors.

Today very little is left of the original site at Hatfield, its association with aviation ceased in 1993 when British Aerospace closed its operation down. Now it has become a large retail park with areas of demolition and development. Large tracts were left unattended for many years and became grasslands. To the delight of local naturalists the only notable flights now are made by the several resident pairs of Short-Eared Owls.

Hatfield was raided by a lone Junkers Ju 88 on 3rd October 1940 which caused this damage. The German bomber was immediately shot down and crash landed not far from its target.

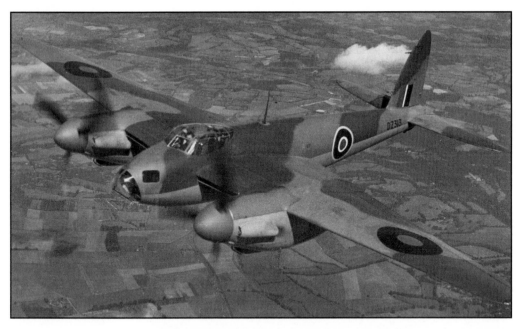

A fine study of a de Havilland Mosquito, one of the most versatile aircraft of World War Two.

HERTFORDSHIRE'S 'WOODEN WONDER' OR 'TIMBER TERROR'- THE DEVELOPMENT OF THE MOSQUITO

One of the most the most famous aviation associations that Hertfordshire can lay claim to is without doubt the development of the de Havilland Mosquito. Some of the finest aeroplanes developed have often excelled in doing things for which they were not originally designed, and this was certainly true in the case of the Mosquito. Originally designed as a bomber, it would later excel in this and just about every other category, particularly that of night fighter.

On 1 March 1940 the first contract was placed for fifty D.H.98 bombers, including prototypes, to be built around the de Havilland proposed specification B.1/40. The design team for this new prototype was led by R E Bishop, R M Clarkson and C T Wilkins. Carrying on the long tradition of entomological aircraft names, the name of Mosquito was suggested and approved at this time.

At one stage de Havilland was asked to concentrate more on production of models such as the Tiger Moth and to shelve the Mosquito production. Had it not been that the Mosquito production utilised non-strategic war materials, chiefly moulded plywood, it may never have been developed.

With the Battle of Britain at its height bombs fell in the vicinity of Hatfield almost daily and during this period 25% of working hours at Hatfield were spent in air raid shelters. On 3 October 1940 a Junkers Ju 88 dropped four bombs that actually fell on the factory with devastating loss of life.

Despite such set-backs the prototype Mosquito (W050) made its first flight on 25 November 1940. Changing priorities of the war now meant that the original order for bombers was changed so that it now comprised of 20 bombers and 30 fighters. This in itself constituted another set-back as numerous parts had already been ordered for the production of 50 bombers as originally agreed. The fighter variant commenced construction at nearby Salisbury Hall and on 15th May 1941 the first prototype fighter took off from a 450 yard grass field, not far from the very hut where it had been constructed.

The Mosquito made its first operational sortie over occupied Europe on 18 September 1941 when a reconnaissance flight was undertaken over France. Squadron Leader Rupert Clerke with his Observer Sergeant Sowerbutts of RAF No 1 PRU took off to investigate Southern France as it was rumoured that German troops were massing for a possible invasion of Spain. On the return flight the electrical generator failed and the batteries ran low, adding to their problems they were bounced by three Me 109s but easily out ran them. On the Home Front the Mosquito night fighter began to take the place of the now war-weary Bristol Blenheims. By late 1942 Mosquitos were operational in ever increasing numbers.

The basic fighter introduced to squadron service in 1942 was the N.F. Mk II, being used largely as a night fighter. It was armed with four 20mm cannon

One of the many women who worked on the Mosquitos applying lacquer coatings to a fuselage.

ventrally and four 0.303 Browning machine guns in the nose and either AI Mk IV or AI Mk V 'arrowhead' radar. The application of the black paint scheme actually slowed the aircraft down by some sixteen miles per hour, although this was not considered critical. Power was delivered by either two Rolls-Royce Merlin 21 or 23 engines.

On the night of 28-29 May 1942 Mosquito NF.IIs scored their first probable night victory. In the following years the Mosquito would account for nearly 600 victories involving enemy aircraft over Britain. Further to this, during the V weapon offensive, just over 600 Doodlebugs were destroyed by Mosquitos in two months.

From 1942 operations included bomber support. During the war in Europe Mosquitos flew 28,000 sorties, dropping 38,000 tons of bombs, for the loss of 193 aircraft (a loss rate of only 0.7%). Of the 466 Mk.IIs produced some had day fighter paint schemes applied, their AI radar removed and saw service in the Mediterranean and North African theatres of war.

From the end of 1942 experience with Mk.II in its day fighter and intruder roles led to the development of the FB.VI. By early 1943 it was clear that the Mosquito had a war load capacity far greater than had been originally estimated and the Mk.VI series was developed with strengthened wing sections for carrying external loads. The full bomb load of 2,000lbs was only carried by the Mk.VI series upgraded with the new Merlin 25 engines. By mid 1943, in addition to its normal RAF duties, the Mk.VI Mosquito was used by Coastal Command in an anti shipping role, being equipped with eight 60lb rockets. More unusual weapons packs included the 57mm Molins Cannon used for ground attack.

An entirely separate line of development from the NF.II model produced a series of night fighter variants primarily used for home defence, The first of these being the NF.XII which was the first aircraft to carry the newly developed concentric AI Radar.

No fewer than 27 variants of the Mosquito were completed during the war years; it carried phenomenal payloads over extreme distances and performed feats beyond the dreams of its designers.

The Mosquito was the ideal aircraft for low level, sometimes roof top height, bombing, such precision raids being made on the Gestapo HQ in Oslo, the Central Registry in The Hague, and Shell House in Copenhagen. One low level raid in particular, the Amiens Raid, made on 18 February 1944 was conducted by Mosquitos based at Hunsdon.

A total of 7,781 Mosquitos were constructed with 6,710 of these during the war years. Of these 6,710 aircraft de Havilland accounted for the building of 5,007 of them. Air forces of thirteen different countries ranging from South Africa to Czechoslovakia flew the Mosquito, surely a creditworthy epitaph to this flying wonder. Production in Britain did not cease until November 1950, the last in the line being an NF. Mk 38 built at Chester.

Note:- Salisbury Hall is now the site of the De Havilland Aircraft Heritage Centre and incorporates the Mosquito Aircraft Museum. Here one can see the original W4050 Mosquito aircraft, as well as numerous Mosquito related artefacts recovered from crash sites. A number of other de Havilland aircraft are exhibited and being restored here.

MOSQUITO COLLISION NEAR ST ALBANS IN 1943.

On 23 August 1943 at approximately 16.50hours two Mosquitoes collided near to Hill End, St Albans. Numerous eye-witnesses were present and watched as the two aircraft banked and flew fast at quite low altitudes. Both then flew separate routes and appeared to circle round, one coming in from the west and one from the east.

At an incredible speed both aircraft were heading straight for each other and every onlooker expected one or both aircraft to sharply bank away, they did not. The sound of the Merlin engines echoed across the surrounding countryside and as the aircraft approached it became a deafening roar. To those watching below it was clear the two aircraft were not going to avoid colliding. Suddenly there was a terrifically sharp 'crack' as they smashed into each other.

Both aircraft instantly disintegrated, smaller pieces of plywood were seen fluttering down. Larger sections cart-wheeled through the sky landing locally, leaving dramatic contorted smoke trails in the air. One section including a fuel tank landed near Hill End and exploded, sending up a plume of thick brown smoke. Near to this lay one of the engines with its battered and twisted yellow tipped propeller blades occasionally visible through the surrounding sheets of flame. The sound of the collision had been heard in nearby Hill End Hospital and a crowd of doctors and nurses ran over to the nearby crash site to assist.

The two aircraft involved were Mosquito Mk.VI fighter fombers HX849 and HX850. The crews were pilot John de Havilland (youngest son of Geoffrey de Havilland) and observer G J Carter and pilot George Gibbins with his observer J H F Scrope. One parachute was seen to open after the collision, but tragically all four crew members were killed.

DEPERDUSSIN DOWN - THE FIRST OF MANY

In 1912 Hertfordshire saw one of the first military air crashes in the world. Indeed it was the very first air crash involving RFC airmen whilst flying on active service.

On 6th September Captain Patrick Hamilton and Lieutenant Atholl Wyness-Stuart took off from Wallingford in Berkshire. Major Brooke Popham was following just behind in a second aircraft. The three aviators that Friday morning were on an important military mission. Aviation was still in its infancy and to test its efficiency these aeroplanes were participating in the East of England Army Manoeuvres of 1912. This involved a mock battle themed upon an invasion of England.

The memorial to the first RFC active service air crash near Wymondley.

As their aircraft approached the Hertfordshire border, Brooke Popham parted company and waved to his two colleagues; he would never see them alive again. He later touched down at the RFC rendezvous point that had been set up at Willian, whilst there he learned of the tragic death of his two colleagues just over a mile away. What had happened on that windy September day?

Due to the novelty of flying machines, numerous people had stopped what they were doing to watch the flimsy Deperdussin pass over Stevenage, the same fascinated curiosity that had first been aroused by Lunardi`s balloon 128 years before.

At about 2,000 feet the little aircraft appeared to be in trouble, small pieces were seen fluttering away and then there was a sharp cracking sound. Having lost power the port wing folded up and the aircraft spun over and continued to break up. Plummeting down, it finally smashed into a thick hedge bordering a meadow.

Mr Walter Brett, landlord of the George and Dragon public house in Graveley, and owner of the meadow saw the incident, 'It dipped and then came a report like a gun', he said. Running over to the crash site he found both airman dead with the wreckage on top of them.

News of the crash spread quickly and caused a sensation. The very next day, 7 September 1912, the incident was national news and even made a pictorial front cover of the Daily Mirror. A few days later, on 12 September, the same newspaper front page carried the full story of their funeral.

People flocked from miles around and began to take souvenirs and mementoes of the tragic event; even the control column assembly was stolen.

Fortunately this looting did not stop the cause of the crash from being established as several key pieces of structure were found. It was ascertained that a connecting rod had fractured within the engine, this in turn had smashed through a section of cowling causing it to detach. As it flew back from the engine area this piece of cowling severed a wire strut. The port wing then began to vibrate and within seconds the wooden wing structure cracked and broke apart. Later on Superintendent George Reed of the Hitchin Police division confirmed that the large section of cowling that severed the wire strut had been found several hundred yards from the crash site.

It was the Graveley air crash which would bring home to the public the dangers of aviation, a herald of the hundreds more fatalities that would occur in just two years time with the outbreak of war.

Both airmen were accorded a heros' funerals, conducted at St Saviours Church in Hitchin, where hundreds of people turned out. So great was the feeling and effect that this incident had that even a special Hymn was composed for the funeral.

Direct with thine all-seeing eye,
Watch each dread journey through the sky,
Through every storm and danger zone,
Bring each brave pilot safely home.

That week a memorial fund was established and in the last week of September a granite obelisk with their names and an inscription was erected near to the meadow where the two men had been killed. The obelisk is still there today on the side of the road and is still a very much known and talked about monument in North Hertfordshire; a tribute to those pioneer aviators of nearly a century ago.

Note: - just four days after this crash another aircraft, a Bristol monoplane also on Army affiliation for these manoeuvres, crashed in Port Meadow, Oxford. Once again two brave pilots were killed: Lieutenant E.H. Hotchkiss and Lieutenant C.A. Bettington.

In this case a piece of metal detached and tore a huge hole in the wing fabric. Two types of monoplane from different manufacturers disintegrating, led to Colonel Seely, then Secretary of State for War, banning the flying of any monoplane by the Military Wing of the RFC. This thoughtless ban was lifted in February 1913, before the decision had damaged the appreciation of aviation in military roles.

THE SCHUTTE LANZ SL-11 DOWN AT CUFFLEY.

At about 11 o'clock on the night of 2 - 3 September 1916, the distant vibrant sound of German Maybach engines was heard once again high in the night sky. Immediately the listeners and the crews of the searchlight batteries knew that the Zeppelins were back, in fact on this night a total of sixteen airships had left their bases in Germany for a mass raid on England. One of these airships was the German Army SL-11 under the command of Wilhelm Schramm, based at Spich in Westphalia, Germany. The SL-11 was an obsolete design; she was an 'e' class Schutte-Lanz and not, as often claimed, a true Zeppelin.

This descriptive inaccuracy has its roots in the British propaganda machine of the time that did indeed list this first enemy airship victory as a 'Zeppelin'. The public had heard of Zeppelins and to them every enemy airship was a Zepp; but a Schutte Lanz? No, Zeppelin it had to be!

Hero of the moment, Second Lieutenant William Leefe-Robinson VC.

The main difference between a true Zeppelin and a Schutte Lanz was that the SL-11's framework was made of wood, braced by wires, unlike the larger Zeppelins that used an aluminium frame. SL-11 had her maiden flight on 2 August 1916, now, barely a month later, she was raiding England.

Schramm crossed the East Coast at the River Crouch and carried on inland, passing over Royston and Hitchin to the northern suburbs of London where searchlights flicked on. Wavering around for a while one beam, then another and another illuminated SL-11 until the ship looked to be supported on a tripod of light.

Second Lieutenant William Leefe-Robinson of 39 Home Defence Squadron RFC had earlier taken off from Suttons Farm at Hornchurch in BE2c No.2693 and was patrolling when he saw SL-11 from some distance away. Descending from 12,000 feet he was about 800 feet below the raider when he opened fire with a drum of alternate loaded Brock-Pomeroy ammunition. Flying the whole length of the airship and raking it with gunfire had no effect. Another drum of ammunition was spent into the side, still to no effect. Leefe-Robinson then dropped back and attacked the rear section of the ship from below, at about 500 feet distance. When the drum was half expired a glow appeared in the rear section and within seconds it was a mass of flames, the resultant glow in the night sky was visible from as far away as Cambridge.

Leefe-Robinson watched as the fabric sections flashed and burned away in seconds, he then fired some red Verey flares and dropped a green parachute flare to mark his victory.

As she fell, the burning SL-11 created a massive ovoid shape of crimson coloured fire, in the midst of which was an almost white incandescent area. A huge cheer went up from sightseers below, who numbered hundreds of thousands; the myth of invincibility that had surrounded these airships had taken its first serious blow. More importantly for the British war effort the seeds of doubt and despair would start to be planted in the minds of every German airship crew from now on.

Leefe-Robinson and the watching public below were not the only ones to see these flares, or the terrible

An artist's impression of SL11's fiery end, produced as a postcard.

glow. Kurt Frankenberg and his crew in Zeppelin L21 were thirty miles to the north over Hitchin and correctly deduced that one of their ships had been hit. Over Tring Oberleutnant Werner Peterson in L32 also witnessed the event, later jettisoning his bombs over Ware. Even nearer that night was Erich Sommerfeldt and his crew in Zeppelin L16; they were just under a mile away and desperately sped off north to escape the glow from the burning SL-11.

The airship had now become a fireball of burning Hydrogen, wood and fabric, and trapped in the inferno was its crew. Floating and spiralling to earth the wreckage fell as a crumpled mass behind the Plough Inn at Cuffley. For some time afterwards sooty smuts of burned envelope fabric and other parts fell from the sky. The smell of burning pervaded for miles around. It is possible that one crew member made an attempt to jump from the burning wreckage, for a leather-clad body was found nearby with femurs smashed upwards and

Souvenirs of SL11 were much prized. Much of the wreck was broken into small pieces and sold to help the Red Cross

collar bones broken. Another body was located whose legs and hands had been burned away.

Leefe-Robinson returned to Suttons Farm at 02.45 hours and later found that he had shot away his own wire machinegun guard and had put several holes in the main spar of his aircraft. Leefe-Robinson became a national hero and received the award of the Victoria Cross within three days of bringing down SL-11. He was only the fifth person ever to receive a VC for action directly linked to the English mainland, but he was the first to be honoured for aerial combat over England.

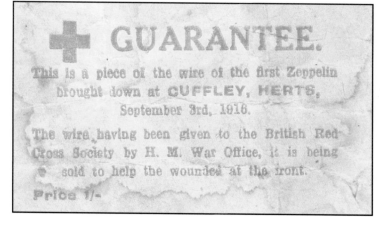

✚ GUARANTEE.

This is a piece of the wire of the first Zeppelin brought down at CUFFLEY, HERTS, September 3rd, 1916.

The wire having been given to the British Red Cross Society by H. M. War Office, it is being sold to help the wounded at the front.

Price 1/-

The crash site at Cuffley attracted thousands of visitors and Leefe-Robinson himself went to examine the result of his efforts that lay strewn across a pasture field in rural Hertfordshire. The authorities later managed to extract many documents and artefacts from the tangled wreckage including tram tickets, money, a brass crucifix, broken Iron Cross and a gold ring thought to belong to Wilhelm Schramm himself. Masses of contorted structural wire lay thickly on the ground and presented quite a task to clear. The Plough Inn sold out of food and drinks by the morning after and was forced to close. From now on the event became known as 'Zeppelin Sunday'.

None of the German airship's crew survived and they were buried in the Mutton Lane cemetery at Potters Bar. In 1966 they were exhumed and reburied at the Cannock Chase Soldatenfriedhof in Staffordshire.

Leefe-Robinson was later shot down in action and made prisoner of war, spending some time in the notorious Holzminden camp. Upon his return to England his resolve weakened and being in a poor physical condition he fell victim to the Influenza Pandemic. He died in his bed on 31 December, 1918, aged just 23. He is buried in Harrow Weald cemetery.

Fragments of SL-11 can still be found today on a wide variety of memorabilia issued at the time of the crash such as sample postcards. Occasionally one sees attributed artefacts for sale on eBay. The largest section I have seen recently was a shattered wooden tip from one of SL-11's large propellers, an item that had been souvenired at the time.

Today a memorial stands in East Ridgeway, Cuffley, commemorating the event and the German crew who lost their lives on that night long ago. Leefe-Robinson's VC was auctioned in 1988 by Christies and realised £99,000, being sold to a private collector. Amongst other personal items in this auction were fragments of SL-11 and a section of fabric cut away from the tail of his BE2c which later crashed, showing the numbers 2693. Monies raised from the auction went to a charity that benefits children.

Contorted metal, charred wood fragments and miles of wire...all that remained of the German airship SL-11. (Courtesy of Ray Rimell)

SL-13 berthed at Wildehausen in 1916; she was the sister-ship of SL-11. (Courtesy of Ray Rimell)

The crew of SL-11 were:-

Hauptmann. Wilhelm Schramm
Obermaschinist. Jakob Baumann
Leutnant. Hans Geitel
Vizefeldwebel. Rudolf Goltz
Feldwebel Leutnant. Karl Paul Hassenmuller
Gefreiter. Bernhard Jeziorski
Untermaschinist. Fritz Jourdan
Untermaschinist. Karl Kachele
Obersteurmann. Fritz Kopischke
Obermaschinist. Friedrich Modinger
Obermaschinist. Reinhold Porath
Unteroffizier. Heinrich Schlichting
Obersteurmann. Rudolf Sendzik
Unteroffizier. Anton Tristram
Oberleutnant der Reserve. Wilhelm Vohdin
Untermaschinist. Hans Winkler

L31 THE POTTERS BAR ZEPPELIN

Shortly after the loss of the SL-11, on the night of 1 - 2 October 1916, eleven airships headed again for England. Of these ships only two, L32 and L31, had been briefed to attack London.

Kapitanleutnant Heinrich Mathy, the 32 year old commander of L31, had left from Nordholz in Northern Germany a few hours before. They passed over Lowestoft at about eight in the evening and steered a deliberate course towards the capital. Mathy was a veteran of many raids over England and was a household name in Germany. Towards Chelmsford it was clear from the erratic bursts of AA fire flashing around them that the outer defences were in a state of readiness, therefore Mathy turned south-west and turned off his engines.

Drifting silently the massive airship passed over the countryside undetected and it was not until the L31 passed over Ware that Mathy gave the order to start up her engines again. Approaching the outer fringes of London searchlights began to waver about in the sky and at least four defence fighters were now airborne. Firing up the engines to full throttle attracted the attentions of several searchlights to their region of the sky and several AA shells burst close by.

Another Zeppelin, L21 commanded by Lt Kurt Frankenberg, was some seventy miles away to the south when its crew saw the searchlights, but clouds then obscured their vision. L31 dropped her entire bomb load and turned west, leaving 36 high explosive and 26 incendiary bombs raining down on Cheshunt. Now relieved of her bomb-load she rose upwards dramatically and nearly escaped.

'The Zeppelin Strafers'
Lieutenant Robinson VC,
Lieutenant Tempest DSO
and Lieutenant Sowrey
DSO.

Second Lieutenant W J Tempest, flying a BE2c from North Weald and also from 39 Home Defence Squadron, was approaching L31 from behind and began firing his first drum of ammunition into the airship's belly. A bright red glow appeared and within a second a huge gout of flame shot out of the nose of the airship. A few seconds later and the airship was a folding mass of white hot aluminium structure surrounded by swirling bursts of flame and burning fabric. The night sky was illuminated for miles around as the flaming wreckage whirled around and downwards, symbolically like a leaf signifying the autumn of the Zeppelins' effectiveness. The glow was also seen by the crew of L21; doing nothing to help their already very dubious morale.

The flaming mass came down in three sections adjacent to Oakmere Park in Potters Bar. The largest of these, the nose section, had impacted an oak

A very popular postcard of the day entitled 'The Fourth !! Super-Zeppelin brought down in flames at Potters Bar, Oct 1st 1916'.

tree, shattering its branches and cloaking it in crumpled aluminium structure. Later this tree became known as The Zeppelin Oak.

Like the SL-11 incident weeks before, numerous people came to see the wreckage and a lucrative trade sprung up selling fragments and charging to get a close-up view the wreckage. The partially buried engines were speedily excavated and taken away for assessment to obtain data relating to high altitude fuel systems. People walked silently over to the corner of a field and for a fee of one shilling could examine the imprint left by a falling body in the soft grass. This was the point where Heinrich Mathy had fallen, he had wrapped a large scarf around his head and jumped. Mathy, the Zeppelin Ace was dead.

The spot where Mathy fell was a meadow behind Cotton Road, but like so many historical sites the area has been the subject of housing development since the 1930s. Some ten years after the event Mathy`s wife visited the scene at Potters Bar where her husband had been killed. Upon seeing that the original wooden cross grave markers were somewhat decayed Frau Mathy complained to the German Embassy. Neither was she happy about a wooden partition that seemed to separate the graves from others in the cemetery. Reaction was swift and the Embassy erected individual headstones and planted shrubs. She did not return for half a century, her last visit taking place in the mid 1970s and Frau Mathy passed away on 23 January 1990.

After his award of the DSO for this action Wulstan Tempest operated with 100 Squadron, flying night-bombers over the Western Front, he left the RAF in 1921 and died in 1966.

Today, adjacent to L31's crash site, are roads named Tempest Avenue and Wulstan Park, named so in tribute to this victorious young pilot. Numerous fragments from L31 are in the local museum and in private collections. An interesting small collection of L31 associated items came up for auction in 2005, included pieces of envelope fabric, melted metal fragments, a bullet, two pieces of German bread and a section of Mathy`s leather coat.

The famous Zeppelin Oak had a complaint made against it because its shattered boughs were considered unsafe, some accounts state it was finally felled in the 1930s others say that it survived into the 1960s. What is sure is that the actual felling was no mean task, as the trunk and boughs were riddled with twisted and flattened pieces of aluminium that snagged the saw repeatedly.

Like the crew of the SL-11, Mathy and his crew-members were exhumed and re-buried Cannock Chase cemetery in Staffordshire in the 1960s.

Interestingly, and rather ironically, the cross on the altar of the Chapel of All Souls, in the Virgin and all Saints church, at Potters manufactured from aluminium salvaged from Nearly ninety years after the crash, in January permission was granted to search Oakmere with metal detectors and three fragments of were found five inches deep in the grassland to the west of the main impact area.

This tangled mass of metal was once Zeppelin L31. It is draped over an oak tree that was to become known as 'The Zeppelin Oak'. (Courtesy of Ray Rimell)

The crew of L31 were:-
Kapitanleutnant. Heinrich Mathy
Maschinistenmaat. Eugen Boundange
Bootsmannmaat. Arthur Budwitz
Obermatrose. Karl Dornbusch
Maschinistenmaat. Nikolaus Hemmerling
Obermaschinistenmaat. Karl Hiort
Segelmachersmaat. Ernst Kaiser
Funkentelegrafieobergast. Ernst Klee
Steuermann. Siegfried Korber
Signalmaat. Gustav Kunischt
Maschinistenmaat. Karl Mensing
Obersteuermannsmaat. Friedrich Peters
Obermatrose. Heinrich Phillipp
Maschinistenmaat. Friedrich Rohr
Maschinistenmaat. Hubert Stender
Maschinist. Joseph Wegener
Leutnant zur See. Jochen Werner
Bootmannsmaat. Heinrich Witthoft
Obermaschinistenmaat. Viktor Woellert

Note: - on Armistice Day (11 November) 1931 a member of the charity Toc-H attended the neglected graves of the Zeppelin crew. Another person was also there, it was Baron Von Nidda, the German Ambassador to Britain. The two men decided to create an annual "Heroes' Day" event in the hope of cementing Anglo-German relations, but by 1933 the celebration had a large

Nazi presence, complete with uniforms and salutes. Several of the other sites where Zeppelins' crew rested also attracted similar attention, but these events were not nearly as organised or as frequent as those at Potters Bar. By 1935 the whole affair, including the service, was being conducted in German and was beginning to create friction with the locals. The Potters Bar Heroes Day that was held in 1939 was the last.

BOMBS DROPPED ON HERTFORDSHIRE DURING WORLD WAR 1

The only offensive items to be dropped on Hertfordshire during this period were from Zeppelins, or other similar German airships such as the Schutte Lanz, but the Gotha and the 'Giant' Zeppelin Staaken aircraft that raided the UK never penetrated as far inland as Hertfordshire. The airships dropped both high explosive and incendiary devices over Hertfordshire.

On 13 October 1915 a Zeppelin appeared over Hertford and was watched by many people as it drifted overhead towards London. An hour or so after this another Zeppelin appeared to the east of Hertford and again drew mass attention. This was L16, that shut off its engines and descended to a lower altitude. At approximately 10 0'clock L16 began dropping her bomb-load over Hertford. In less than two minutes 30 incendiary and 14 high explosive bombs hit the town. In this period nine people were killed, 15 people wounded and 110 buildings destroyed or damaged. Bombs had fallen from Hartham, Bull Plain, Mill Bridge, and Old Cross, finishing with two explosions in the grounds of the hospital. Later, L31 jettisoned her bomb-load of 36 high explosive and 26 incendiary bombs on Cheshunt in October 1916.

The first enemy bomb in World War One to be dropped in Brickendon fell in a field at Highfield Farm, incredibly some quarter of a century later this same field was the recipient of the first enemy bomb to be dropped in this area during the Second World War.

The size and types of Zeppelin bombs varied, the most common bomb load being a mix of 50kg-60kg high explosive and 3kg incendiary bombs. There were much larger bombs used on occasion over Britain, as well as the smaller spherical shaped grenades of approx 2kg to 62kg size. It would seem from records that Hertfordshire mainly received bombs from standard bomb loads and types, and nothing larger.

On the night of 2-3 September 1916 high explosive and incendiary bombs fell at London Colney, South Mimms and a single high explosive bomb fell in Osborne Road at Potters Bar. In 1916 a Zeppelin passed over the village of Weston, dropping a small high explosive bomb that landed in a meadow adjacent to the church. Little damage was done apart from some turf dispersal in the meadow from a three feet deep crater some six feet across, traces of which can just about still be seen today. This small crater would seem to indicate this was a grenade rather than a bomb.

On the night that the SL-11 was shot down, 2-3 October 1916, Zeppelin L16 (the airship which nearly a year before had devastated Hertford) captained by Erich Sommerfeldt dropped several bombs on Essendon. These resulted in the deaths of two sisters Frances and Eleanor Bamford and some considerable damage to the church. Later in 1917 a unidentified German airship dropped several bombs on Hertford.

On the night of 19-20 October 1917, eleven 'Height Climber' Zeppelins set out to raid England. The majority became disorientated by high headwinds leading the crew of L55 to drop bombs on Hitchin and Hatfield when they believed they were over Birmingham.

Not easily identified as a bomb, these rope and tar incendiary bombs or 'fire pots' were often found unexploded (left) or burnt-out (right).

Just occasionally the smaller incendiary devices and grenades dropped are still discovered; one being found in the corner of a barn at Weston in the 1970s. Since they don't resemble a conventional bomb shape, more a handled rope-bound bucket in the case of incendiaries and spherical for grenades, one can assume in many cases they were not recognised for what they were, indeed an elderly Hertfordshire gentleman used an incendiary device as a doorstop for over 60 years. Arriving home from the pub worse for wear some nights he would kick the 'doorstop' out of the way, to roll off a short distance down the path….. until a relative recognised it for what it was.

World War Two - Luftwaffe

SHARK'S MOUTH AT KIMPTON
FRIDAY 30TH AUGUST 1940

Aircraft:	**Crew**
Messerschmitt Bf 110 C. M8+MM 4./ZG 76	Oberfeldwebel Georg Anthony (27) (Pilot)
Werke Nummer 3615	killed
Location:	Unteroffizier Heinrich Nordmeier
Kimpton, Hertfordshire	(Bordfunker) severely injured.
Date/Time:	
16.30 hours, 30th August 1940	

**Shot down by Flying Officer Ludwik Paszkiewicz of No.303 Squadron
and Pilot Officer B J Wicks of No.56 Squadron.**

On Friday 30 August 1940, the 'shark's mouth' emblazoned twin-engined Messerschmitt Bf 110s took off once more from France. At the controls of the one aircraft marked M8+MM was 27 year old Oberfeldwebel Georg Anthony. He was already a seasoned and experienced veteran and, together with Nordmeier as his radio operator and gunner, had actively participated in the French campaign.

In the Battle of France Anthony had led several daring and well-executed attacks on French aeroplanes, shooting down several Morane-Saulnier fighters. Anthony was frequently to be found embroiled in desperate aerial combats; as well as achieving a reputation, he appeared to be well on the way to becoming one of the war's earliest ZG76 aces.

On this day his Messerschmitt was to act as one of the many escort fighters for the Heinkel He 111s of Kampfgeschwader 53.

Many of ZG76's Me 110s were adorned with a 'Shark's Mouth' or as the Luftwaffe called it the *Haifische*.

A Luftwaffe mechanic works on the nose-mounted guns of an Me 110.

At about 14.15 hours an estimated 300 enemy aeroplanes were approaching the Thames Estuary and Kent coast. From these areas they divided into smaller groups and proceeded inland. Attacks were made on Debden, Biggin Hill and other significant aerodromes.

One group of KG53 Heinkels and their Me 110 escorts, initially heading for Radlett aerodrome, became detached. This group penetrated as far inland as Luton where they found and bombed a prime target, the Vauxhall Motor Works. The Heinkels of KG53 released 59 bombs onto the factory and surrounding area of Luton. The engineering section of the works was very badly hit; one direct hit killed seven people sheltering beneath a stairway. In Luton twenty people were killed, 174 injured - 49 seriously.

Despite the extent of the damage the plant was back in production within six days but it took longer for Bomb Disposal to clear and render safe the many UXBs that lay in the district.

Leaving their target shrouded in smoke and dust the raiding force turned east and headed towards the Thames Estuary and home. Two aircraft of the Vauxhall raid were lost on the way to the target. One fell at Kimpton, the other, also an Me 110, which was coded M8+BM crashed into a sewage works at Enfield in Essex.

One eyewitness to this attack was living in Stevenage at the time and said, "You could see the German aeroplanes, they were ever so high. They looked like mere specks in the blue sky, if you listened carefully you could just hear feint sounds of machine gun fire." Other witnesses spoke of hearing the ominous fluctuating drone of the approaching German formation.

COMBAT

On a training flight in the area at this time were the Hurricane pilots of No.303 Squadron from Northolt. The Polish pilots literally stumbled upon the enemy aeroplanes. They took no time in getting stuck into the escorts and their bomb laden Heinkels.

The fact that 303 Squadron was training on this day intercepting six RAF Bristol Blenheims when they stumbled across this raid is immortalised in the film 'The Battle of Britain'. The point in the film where the Polish pilots dive away (despite being told to stay in formation) to attack amidst lots of Polish chatter on the R/T, is supposed to represent this action over Hertfordshire. Paszkiewicz was unable to contact Squadron Leader Kellet who led the training flight and, not wanting to miss this superb opportunity, he peeled away to attack.

Later Paszkiewicz was officially reprimanded and, in the next breath, informed that he and the squadron were now considered fully operational.

The King talks to Polish pilots of 303 Sqn. L-R; S/L Urbanowicz, F/Lt R S Forbes, F/Lt Ludwik Paszkiewicz and F/Lt Walery Zak

WITNESSES

Far below the battle farm workers and local villagers witnessed a thrilling dogfight involving numerous aeroplanes wheeling and diving, machinegun fire was loud.

One eyewitness counted twenty-seven German aeroplanes in formation, with three RAF fighters attacking them. Mrs G Sharnbrook had a superb view of the combat being played out above her, she remarked how the, "British

Fighters looked like angry wasps going in to attack." Frequently there would be a sharp flash and glint of light as the bright sun reflected off the cockpits of friend and foe alike.

PC Pavett had watched the entire dogfight from a distance and as the noise got louder and louder he placed his wife and family in the garden air raid shelter.

The 'twin-engined bomber' that Ludwik Paszkiewicz had singled out over Stevenage was the Me110 being flown by Georg Anthony. Trying desperately to shake off his determined attacker Anthony descended sharply. Twisting and turning at full throttle the Messerschmitt could not get escape. Small fragments of fuselage became detached from the Messerschmitt amid a series of flashes and puffs of white smoke.

Banking sharply, a furious and accurate burst of gunfire caused the starboard wing tip of Anthony's Messerschmitt to disintegrate. This ripped away and fluttered back past the attacking Hurricane. Unceasingly the De Wilde ammunition from the Hurricane flashed and sparked as it hit M8+MM. The .303 rounds either punched small neat holes or great paint splintered ragged holes through which the air stream whistled and shrieked as M8+MM jinked from side to side.

Above the screaming noise from the port engine Anthony and Nordmeier could hear the clattering sounds from damaged and detaching sections of their aeroplane. The starboard engine of the Messerschmitt was now put out of action, and from it a thick streak of flame and black smoke began to line the summer sky. Surprisingly, despite being seriously damaged, Anthony still managed through sheer determination to keep his aeroplane in horizontal flight.

Paszkiewicz then saw another Hurricane draw alongside him and also fire on 'his' target. Nordmeier jettisoned the rear cockpit canopy and baled out over the Hertfordshire countryside.

On the ground Jack Marshall and Alf Symons stopped work to watch

the dogfight. Up above they watched the final attack delivered on what they concluded was an 'already seriously done-for Jerry'. Almost immediately the German aircraft rolled over, assumed an inverted position, and began to plummet earthwards. Picking up incredible speed further sections detached and fluttered away, lost briefly from sight in the rushing smoke plume. The tail unit briefly swung sideways and then snapped off and spun away under the pressure from terrific forces. The tattered remains of M8+MM fell down through the bright summer sky with a terrible whining scream.

Just before impact the broken Messerschmitt seemed to level out, and then it smashed through a row of mature Elm trees. These huge trees sheared off the remains of the wings outboard of each engine, shattered the fuselage and totally smashed the cockpit.

In a flurry of shattered wood, twigs, leaves and smoke the remainder of the wreckage smashed through into a corner of a field bordering Claggybottom Lane. The nose section compressed in a second as it smashed into the ground, instantly ramming compressed clay three feet up each cannon gun barrel. The two hot engines then hit the ground smashing off their propeller bosses and shearing off some blades before punching eight feet into the stone laden clay. These engines took the nose and part of the cockpit section down with them.

One man standing over half a mile away said his feet felt the vibration of the impact. Immediately the Messerschmitt exploded and a huge ball of orange flame shot up, followed by a thick billowing black smoke cloud.

Just over a thousand feet above the shattered tranquillity of this English countryside scene Wicks, pilot of the second Hurricane, performed a victory role. Georg Anthony, the pilot, had stayed in the cockpit until impact. Perhaps

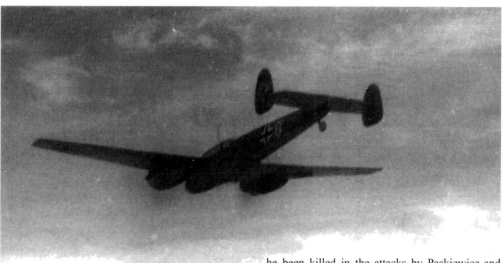

he been killed in the attacks by Paskiewicz and Wicks, had been wounded, or simply could not release t h e canopy due to damage.

PC Pavett watched a body tumble from the sky until a parachute opened at a low height and drifted down across the fields near Tallents Farm. He went off in the direction he assumed the parachutist to have come down and found Nordmeier, who had hit the ground heavily and whose spine was broken in several places. PC Pavett reported that he was a tall blonde haired fellow; he was still alive, had a large bloodied gash on his forehead, but was barely conscious.

Being nervous that the German could be shamming his consciousness PC Pavett disarmed him, released his harness and had him conveyed to Kimpton on a stretcher. Amongst some of the items 'liberated' from the pockets of the lucky-to-be-alive radio operator was a quantity of British manufactured cigarettes. One wonders if these cigarettes may have originated from the supplies left behind during the Dunkirk Evacuation.

When he arrived at Kimpton he was attended by Dr Probyn and then conveyed by ambulance to a nearby searchlight unit situated in Whitwell.

CRASH INVESTIGATION

Having completed the task of handing Nordmeier over to the military authorities PC Pavett, along with four members of the Home Guard, decided to make his way to the crash site. As he neared the elm trees he could see a large number of people had gathered next to the smoking crater. These included another member of the constabulary and some more Home Guard members, who were doing their best to cordon off the crater from sightseers and souvenir hunters.

When the flames and smoke had subsided, partially as a result of a Fire Brigade team in attendance, a crater could be seen. This was some twenty feet across and five feet deep. From the depths protruded a mass of mangled metal, wiring and about six inches of one buried propeller blade.

It would seem that as the remains of M8+MM had only penetrated some eight feet into the flinty clay of the field, the impact velocity having been considerably reduced by collision with the trees. In the crater could be seen the bloodied and tattered remains of the lower half of Georg Anthony's body. Scattered around the crater were large sections of wing structure and fuselage fragments.

Looking up into the shattered top section of an elm tree someone noticed a large section of uniformed torso. Also in the vicinity, to the horror of locals, lay a flying boot complete with a foot inside and a head minus its scalp, the scalp of ginger coloured hair was recovered later. Near to the hedge one souvenir seeker is reported to have picked up a pack of coloured pencils.

As the crash scene was investigated in depth it is rumoured that someone checking inside an adjacent hollow tree trunk discovered a 'Blunderbus' possibly secreted there by a highway man or suchlike, two centuries before.

Another person, perhaps a member of the constabulary, caught a man making off with Georg Anthony's side arm pistol that he had found in the lane.

Later that afternoon, with the road sealed off, PC Pavett began discreetly collecting the human remains from within and around the crater. These included the quite macabre sight of two clenched severed hands in a nearby hedgerow. He assumed they were in such a condition due to the pilot strenuously pulling on the control column.

Collecting as much as he could find, which came to nearly three quarters of a grain sack, he placed the remains at the bottom of his garden. Here they remained for several days until, attracting so many blowflies, he decided to convey them in a tea chest to Hitchin for military funeral preparations. PC Pavett later confirmed that as far as he knows no identity tag was found with the remains.

Back at the crash scene a photographer from the Herts Pictorial newspaper had arrived and took a considerable number of exposures. These included some posed shots with Home Guard members around the wreckage.

One photograph purports to show the tail section, but examination clearly shows the Balkankreuz marking from one of the crumpled wings. The newspaper reported that, due to the violent nature of the crash, it was not possible to ascertain what type of enemy aeroplane this was. It was also indicated that the explosion was caused by detonating bombs, clarifying the lack of knowledge as bombs were not carried on escort Me 110s at that stage of the war.

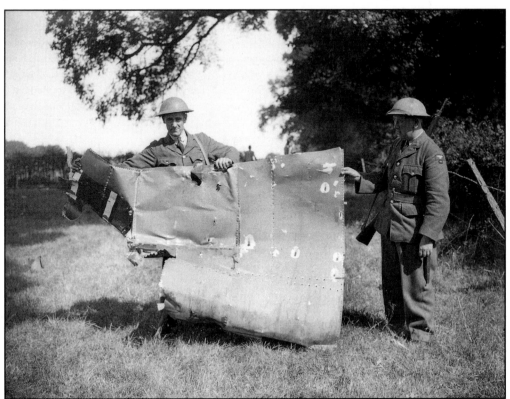

It was noted that around the crater's edge, and also in the lane, were found some shredded sections of flight map, evidence it was said that the pilot attempted to destroy the map as he fell.

In addition to this a partially deployed parachute was taken as evidence that he had made some attempt to vacate the stricken aeroplane. Whilst both indeed could be true, it is more likely the violence of the impact created these issues.

One week after the crash the pitiful remains of Georg Anthony were accorded a military funeral, the cortege passing through the streets of Hitchin. His coffin, draped in a swastika flag, was placed on a wheeled carriage and pulled through the crowd-lined streets which led to the cemetery.

The RAF attended the funeral, whether this included Paskiewicz and Wicks I have not been able to establish. One hopes it was them attending to pay their respects to a gallant but fallen foe. The remains of Georg Anthony still rest in Hitchin cemetery to this day, unlike many of his Luftwaffe colleagues he was not exhumed and re-buried at Cannock Chase in the 1960s.

For days after the crash people visited the site to look for souvenirs, items recovered ranged from small twisted pieces of alloy to live cannon shells. Finally a Queen Mary low-loader vehicle arrived and assisted in the removal of all the large surface wreckage. Three days later a young lad climbed to the top of one of the elm trees to grab a piece of the Messerschmitt that was still stuck up there. As he tore it down he could see that it was riddled with bullet holes. Peter Stokes, a local lad, managed to raise five shillings and seven pence for the Spitfire fund by selling pieces to family and friends.

Perhaps the most remarkable souvenir to be taken was that removed by Mr Ansell soon afterwards. Visiting the crash site on the evening it happened he

Complete with swastika flag draped coffin, the funeral cortege of Georg Anthony passes through Hitchin. It is rumoured women could be seen crying at the event.

managed to take home a huge section of fuselage bearing the Balkankreuz. He kept this for many years until it was sold to a passing scrap merchant.

Mr Ansell later wrote, "On the afternoon of Friday 30 August 1940 a German plane was shot down by our fighters and crashed at Claggybottom near Kimpton. At that time I lived at Diamond End and went to the scene within an hour of the crash. One of the crew managed to bale out and was captured, but one was killed. I saw part of his body hanging in a tree. In the evening I returned to the scene and took part of the fuselage, which included the 'Iron Cross' which I kept as a souvenir for many years."

On that evening as the strength of the summer sun ebbed a strange creaking noise emanated from the depths of the crater, even after several hours the engines of M8+MM were still cooling down.

BRIEF BIOGRAPHIES

Ludwik Paszkiewicz

The Hurricane pilot who delivered the initial attack on the Kimpton Me110 was Polish fighter pilot Ludwik Paszkiewicz. He was an experienced flyer, however several weeks prior to this combat he had been involved in a landing

accident in Hurricane P3645, which had been wrecked as a result. Fortunately he had been unhurt.

On 27 September 1940 Hurricane L1696, coded RF-M, smashed into the ground on Crowhurst Farm at Borough Green, Kent. The young pilot killed in the impact was Ludwik Paskiewicz.

Many years later aviation archaeologists were to excavate the impact point of L1696. Here they recovered numerous artefacts including a propeller blade that was subsequently donated to the Sikorsky Museum in London. Ludwik Paskiewicz is buried in Northwood cemetery.

Pilot Officer B.J.Wicks

The second attacker was Pilot Officer B J Wicks of No.56 Squadron based at North Weald.

Wicks also had a colourful flying career. On the 25 August 1940 he had been flying over the Thames Estuary and had shot down  an Me 109E-4.

This Me 109 was piloted by Unteroffizier Buschmeyer who succeeded in baling out.

Many years later The London Air Museum excavated the site and recovered an intact DB601A engine and the two wing mounted 20mm MGFF cannons.

On 26 August the tables turned. Wicks had been flying Hurricane V7340 over Canterbury when he was bounced by an Me 109. Becoming embroiled in combat Wicks was shot down, baling out successfully. His Hurricane crashed into the river Stour near Grove Ferry, Upstreet, Kent.

On Monday 30 September 1940 Wicks was flying Hurricane P3870 over Portland, where he intercepted a Dornier 215. Despite several other pilots reporting engagements with Dornier 215s that day, this is probably a case of misidentification and the aeroplane involved was more than likely a Dornier Do 17.

This Dornier gave very accurate return fire which damaged Wicks' Hurricane. This resulted in a forced landing at Warmwell aerodrome. Wicks was unhurt and the aeroplane deemed repair worthy. Wicks was at least to survive The Battle of Britain.

Pilot Officer B J Wicks of No.56 Squadron

66 YEARS ON

The current landowner excavated the buried remains of M8+MM in 1982. Amongst items recovered were both engines in excellent condition, although as to be expected the starboard bore evidence of fire damage and bullet strike marks on the casing. Impacted clay was rammed into every engineered crevice on these engines and both had adherent orange coloured clay. Orange coloured because the heat from each engine had fired the surrounding clay.

Both undercarriage assemblies were also found, along with a much-compressed radiator, tubing, rubber pipes, manufacturer's plates, both propeller bosses and masses of compressed airframe. One of the propeller bosses had a small section of propeller blade protruding from it and on this can be seen traces of red paint. The forward firing 20mm cannons were found still in their shrouding blast tubes.

The landowner was also extremely fortunate to locate a splendid brown blue and gold coloured enamel engine badge from the Niedersachsige Motoren Werke at Braunschweig. This showed the NMW logo with a walking lion above it, a truly evocative little artefact relating back to the height of The Battle of Britain.

Of the crash site today there is little evidence, the odd green or grey painted fragment of airframe is occasionally visible in the plough soil from the roadside. Of the once magnificent elms that lined the field and lane there remains just rotten ivy clad stumps, barely discernible amongst the roadside vegetation. Several years ago I checked one of these stumps and there in the leaf mould was a large lump of Daimler Benz engine casting complete with exhaust valve. Further rummaging around revealed other sections and pieces of corroded skinning. I wondered if I had discovered the long forgotten stash of a 1940s schoolboy.

So what was then a quiet leafy lane with thick hedges in 1940 is now a windswept open lane across arable farmland. In sixty-six years the scenery has changed dramatically, mainly attributable to Dutch elm disease in the late 1960s. Most people passing along the lane know nothing of the carnage that occurred here on that hot summer afternoon back in 1940, but hopefully there are a few who for curiosities sake still go and look over the bleak fields and nettle filled lane edge to ponder.

A manufacturer's plate from the tail fin of the Kimpton Messerschmitt.

Perhaps they, like me, close their eyes for a few seconds and imagine shouted voices from across the fields combined with the irritated calls of a Yellowhammer, and think of the summer tranquillity brutally interrupted some six decades before.

THE HUNSDON HEINKEL

FRIDAY 30TH AUGUST 1940

Aircraft:	Crew:
Heinkel He111 H-2 A1+CR 7. /KG53	Gefreiter R.Reiss (Killed).
Location:	Gefreiter L.Stilp (Mortally wounded
Hunsdon aerodrome	died same day)
Time:	Feldwebel W.Kusserow. (Minor injuries)
16.30 hours	Feldwebel G. Distler. (Minor injuries)
	Leutnant E. Fischbach. (Uninjured)

Shot down by- Lieutenant W H Rhodes-Moorhouse, Pilot Officer H T Gilbert,

Sergeant R N Taylor and Pilot Officer T Grier of 'B' Flight No.601 Squadron.
KG 53 lost five Heinkel He 111s on this raid. The scheduled target for this particular aeroplane
was Radlett aerodrome.

COMBAT

During its low level flight the Heinkel was pounced upon by Hurricanes of 'B' Flight No.601 Squadron. The pilots known to have attacked this aeroplane were:- Lieutenant W H Rhodes-Moorhouse, Pilot Officer H T Gilbert, Sergeant R N Taylor and Pilot Officer T Grier. In the initial attacks the starboard engine was put out of action and a long thin stream of white smoke trailed backwards from the blazing Heinkel, it was clearly doomed. It rapidly lost height, but the pilot managed to level out.

This was seen by the Hurricane pilots and so the attacks resumed, the fuselage and tailfin were absolutely peppered by bullet holes. During these attacks Gefreiter Reiss was killed outright and Gefreiter Stilp mortally wounded. Losing height still further the Heinkel approached the area of Hunsdon aerodrome from the east with the Hurricanes literally stacking up waiting to attack from behind.

WITNESSES

One eyewitness said, "the attacks did not cease until the Heinkel had crash landed", and that, "those RAF boys must have been really pissed off with this one!" He also stated that for a few seconds bullets were hitting the ground all around his house and that one round smashed a hole in one of his windows. Incredibly it was only in the 1990s that this cracked and holed windowpane had been replaced.

Another eyewitness saw no less than five Hurricanes behind and slightly above the Heinkel. To all watching from below and in the air the Heinkel was definitely doomed, with the starboard engine already out of action and the port engine engulfed in flames. However this played no part in reducing the unrelenting attacks from the Hurricane pilots who pressed home attack after attack.

After the combat you could literally follow a trail of 0.303 cartridges across the fields up to where the Heinkel lay. It is also reported that one of the Hurricanes landed nearby and the pilot walked over to the Heinkel wreck, whereupon a member of the Home guard presented him with the pilot's pistol.

Geoff Roberts saw the Heinkel come down and still has a small, once molten, section from one of the MG15 machinegun saddle drums taken at the time. Geoff and his brothers were amongst the very first people to get to the wrecked Heinkel. Later a guard who had been posted there asked the boys if they would like a souvenir, each brother was given a piece of metal. One brother did considerably better than the others as, after hacking and cutting at the thin tail stabiliser alloy, the guard presented him with a fine wartime trophy - the compete swastika marking. Sadly as in many cases most of these trophies were lost in the 1950s and only Geoff's saddle drum section has survived to this day.

John Clarke also saw the flaming Heinkel coming down, passing no more than 30 feet over the church spire at Gilston. He confirms the huge amount of fired 0.303 cases that lay about from the combat; he used many of them as 'toy soldiers'.

Hunsdon aerodrome at this time was undergoing construction and the pilot of the Heinkel managed to land the crippled machine, which was well and truly alight, between two rows of derelict cars. Eyewitness to this landing all state that it was 'perfect' and given that the plane was on fire, and still under fire, it does seem that the pilot was very skilled to pull this off. The cars had been here for some while and were probably placed there to hinder potential enemy landings during an invasion attempt.

The pilot's view from inside the cockpit of a Heinkel He 111.

Landing in a hail of bullets, the Heinkel stopped and continued to burn. A fire also broke out halfway down the fuselage, burning away a section about twelve feet in length.

Construction workers and soldiers from the South Lancs Regiment ran towards the enemy machine. They discovered the body of Gefreiter Reiss inside. Gefreiter Stilp was removed severely wounded and was continually asking for 'a glass of water'. Stilp was to die later that day in Hertford Hospital.

Of the rest of the crew Kusserow and Distler both had minor wounds, only Leutnant Fischbach remained unwounded. The entire crew, including the body of Gefreiter Reiss, was firstly taken to Hunsdon Rectory where Mrs Wilson, the Rector's, wife administered to the wounded as best she could. Mr Wilson, the Rector, remembered that the pilot spoke incredibly good English and said that he had flown seventeen missions over England in this same aeroplane.

He noticed with some distaste that when the Military Police arrived that evening to take away the surviving crew, one of them removed the Iron Cross from the pilot's tunic and pocketed it. The cloth breast eagle was also removed from the pilot's tunic and is currently held in a private collection. Originally this cloth eagle had been given to a young wartime evacuee called Peter Wright, along with a piece of ripped shirt or tunic belonging to one of the crew.

The two dead crewmembers were buried next day, Gefreiter Stilp in St Dunstans Churchyard at Hunsdon and Gefreiter Reiss in Hertford Cemetery. Since that day both have been exhumed and now rest at Cannock Chase Block 5 graves 244 and 243.

'Willie' Rhodes-Moorhouse

Pilots of No.601 Squadron line up by the tailplane of one of their Hurricanes.

CRASH INVESTIGATION

The Heinkel although severely shot up only partially burned out. Later examination revealed an armament of four MG15 machine guns and, more unusually, a sub-machinegun. In the event of a crash-landing in England some crews did opt to carry machineguns in the event that they may need to defend themselves. It was decided to place the reasonably intact aeroplane on display at Hunsdon aerodrome, where it stayed for five weeks before being removed.

This lengthy stay allowed many eyewitnesses to make notes on markings and colour schemes. The letter 'C' of the aeroplane's code appeared on the upper surfaces of both port and starboard wingtips. The numbers 2624 were stencilled on the rudder, below this were seventeen white stripes representing war flights, as indicated by the pilot. The overall camouflage was reported to have been 'orange, green and dark brown' applied in the standard Luftwaffe splinter pattern.

BRIEF BIOGRAPHIES

'Willie' Rhodes-Moorhouse

One of the attacking pilots that day, 'Willie' already had a prestigious connection with flying, his father was William Barnard Rhodes-Moorhouse had been the recipient of the first VC awarded for aerial warfare. Sadly this was posthumously awarded as he was killed on 26 April 1915.

His only son 'Willie' carried on his father's desire to fly and obtained his pilot's licence at the age of 16. He later served with 601 Squadron in France where he scored two kills. In the early stages of the Battle of Britain he scored three more kills.

On 30 July 1940 he was awarded the DFC. On 11 August 1940 he destroyed two Me 109s and would add another five more kills to his tally. Like so many young airmen of the day his life was cut tragically short; when flying a patrol on 6 September 1940 Me 109s 'bounced' his Hurricane and he was shot down over Tunbridge Wells.

One of only two known relics of the Hunsdon Heinkel; a cloth breast eagle removed from the pilot's tunic.

66 YEARS ON

The area of the crash site was briefly examined in the early 1990s. It appears that the impact point is near the intersection of the two wartime runways. The Imperial War Museum holds a section of fuselage from this Heinkel. The item was salvaged by 334 Searchlight Battery, Royal Artillery and can be seen in case 53 in the Second World War galleries

The author would like to draw attention to the local research work of author and historian Denis Sharp, as well as eye-witness Geoff Robertson, who supplied much additional information on this incident.

RAIDER AT THORLEY

THURSDAY 19TH SEPTEMBER 1940

Aircraft:	Crew:
Heinkel He 111 P-2 G1+GL 3./KG55	Unteroffizier H. Pohl. (Killed)
Location:	Unteroffizier W. Goliath. (Killed)
Thorley Wash, Thorley.	Feldwebel T. Alpers. (Killed)
Time:	Unteroffizier W. Gertz (Seriously wounded).
23.40 hours	

At 23.40 hours on Thursday 19 September, 1940, Hertfordshire received its third crashed German aeroplane, and second example of the Heinkel He 111.

COMBAT

Whilst flying over its London target this machine had allegedly received a direct hit by Anti Aircraft fire which may have damaged the tail surfaces. The Heinkel pilot flew on and began to lose height, but the aircraft disintegrated in the air just before impact and finally come to rest in Thorley Wash.

CRASH INVESTIGATION

The Heinkel crashed in marshy ground at Thorley Wash near Bishop's Stortford and was very badly damaged. The tail unit had broken away to land near Latchmore Bank. The wings and fuel tanks lay on the side of the main A11 road, whilst the fuselage, engines and cockpit came down near the river. There were no witnesses to the final impact, but many heard the growling, throbbing, drone of the aeroplane's engines as it approached the area.

It thumped down into a waterlogged area at the side of the River Stort, and much of the wreckage sank in the reedy margins. Sections of fuselage caught fire and the sound of exploding ammunition could be heard.

Manufacturer's plate from the Heinkel that crashed at Thorley Wash.

A He 111 of KG55 showing the mottled and patchy night-time distemper camouflage for operations during the Blitz on Britain.

Mr Clark, who worked as a stoker at the B/S gas works, was on fire watch that night and clearly heard the plane come down. The morning afterwards he took his dog for a walk and came across Unteroffizier Willi Gertz, who had a badly broken ankle, in a stubble field. Gertz pulled out his pistol and offered it to Mr Clark who threw it away out of reach and was collected the same day by a policeman. The injured airman was then taken to Haymeads Hospital, some saw that he was taken there on a detached farm gate serving as a stretcher.

Other locals believe that Unteroffizier Gertz landed very heavily, coming down in the local sewage farm, with only a partially deployed parachute, yet others believe that he came down in a wood near St Giles church at Great Hallingbury. Later on in the war several German prisoners were released to work in the gas works with Mr Clark, incredibly one of them was Willi Gertz.

The parachute of the injured airman was retrieved later that day to make clothing. According to Mrs Monk the stitching of its seams were incredibly difficult to unpick.

Reg Parnell remembers that the wings of the Heinkel had detached and lay some distance from the fuselage. The tail section had also broken away and lay several hundred feet away. The tail unit appeared to have a mass of wire around it that was believed at the time to be from a parachute and cable rocket device used to bring down low flying enemy aeroplanes, but it was an electricity cables that the tail unit had become entangled in.

A boy on the scene early next morning stared in silent thought at one of the arms of a crewmember sticking out awkwardly from a clump of disturbed reeds. Closer examination found that the arm still had a ticking watch attached, but he could not bring himself to remove it, and left it there. Days later when the main wreckage, which due to its location was very difficult to retrieve, had been removed he returned armed with a long garden rake. Plunging it into the crater time and time again he pulled out bomb fuzing panels and cables, cockpit instruments, pumps and a whole host of interesting items.

On his second visit he thrust the rake deep down and hit a large solid object, carefully tracing its contours he concluded that it was a very large bomb. He decided against any further recovery operations! Other schoolchildren arrived at the site and clambered over the broken Heinkel's remains. Several took fragments of perspex, fashioned them into key-fobs and sold them at school.

The bomb load (Incendiary and HE bombs) was still on board and no attempt had been made to jettison it. This might indicate that the crew did not know how badly damaged their aeroplane had been by AA fire. There are accounts of an explosion and a medium sized crater near to the River Stort that may be an indication that at least one large calibre bomb exploded upon impact.

Sid Oxborrow was another local lad who went to the water filled crater and found some incendiary bombs and pieces of twisted alloy. Sid took a large piece of aluminium as a souvenir, which his father later made into a spade for him. The night before he and his family had been standing outside their air raid shelter watching the 'fireworks' of the Blitz on London and saw the flash and glow of the exploding Heinkel. Other large parts that lay in the vicinity of the crash site were an engine block and a large main undercarriage tyre that was still inflated.

Bryan South remembers bouncing about on this large inflated tyre and playing on the engine block in the 1940s and thinks both may have been c o v e r e d over during anti-flood river bank reinforcement. Up until

a Heinkel He 111
of KG55

Luftwaffe ground crew pose with the deadly cargo destined for Britain.

the 1960s the tip of a propeller blade could still be seen protruding from the marsh every winter when the reeds died away. Rumours also exist that the tail fin, still bearing the swastika, had lain outside a local house for many years.

66 YEARS ON

In the years afterwards the site became overgrown with willow trees and remained undisturbed until the local water authority dug some ditches to assist drainage. Apparently a few fragments of alloy were recovered, but no sign of the large bomb.

I have managed to search the site and found four pieces of alloy, one was quite a large chunk of casing bearing a BAL manufacturer's stamp. Apart from these the only other artefacts originating from this crash are those taken by the local lads who visited the crash site.

All three airmen killed in the crash rest in Saffron Walden cemetery, not having been re-interred in Cannock Chase. There is a local legend that on occasions the ghost of one of the crew has been seen standing in an adjacent garden looking down upon the marshy land where his Heinkel ended its days. This would be disputed by the cynical, but what cannot be disputed is that several feet down in this marshland lies a very large bomb.

The author would like to draw attention to the local research work of author and Thorley historian Bill Hardy.

65

THE HATFIELD JUNKERS 88

THURSDAY 3RD OCTOBER 1940

Aircraft:	Crew:
Junkers Ju 88 A-1 W.Nr. 4136 3Z+BB Stab	Oberleutnant Siegward Fiebig (Pilot).
1./KG77	Feldwebel Heinz Ruthof
Location:	(Air Gunner and Bomb Aimer).
Eastend Green, Hertingfordbury.	Oberfeldwebel Erich Goebel
Time:	(Radio Operator and Navigator).
11.40 hours	Unteroffizier Kurt Seiffert (Air Gunner).
	(All Uninjured).

The crew had taken off from Laon aerodrome In France at 09.40 hours, briefed to attack Reading. However the weather on this October morning was very poor with persistent drizzle and low cloud. Whilst over England the crew in became rapidly disorientated. After flying around for some time they spotted a break in the cloud, through which they dropped and levelled out in an attempt to find a landmark to get some idea of where they were. The time now was exactly 11.23 hours and the Junkers was approaching Hatfield rapidly from the South east. As they levelled out they could not believe their luck when a large and tempting target appeared in front of them. Within seconds they were right over Hatfield aerodrome, but on the ground below the response was rapid.

Extensive damage was caused to de Havilland`s at Hatfield by the bombs of a single Junkers Ju 88 from KG77 on the 3rd October 1940.

COMBAT

The ground defences opened up almost immediately with everything from Bofors to mounted machine guns. Fiebig swung the Junkers in a wide circular flight path around the aerodrome perimeter. Then he began a dive-bombing run, releasing six bombs (some sources say four). These were released at such low altitude that each of them bounced off the tarmac apron of the airfield, leaving behind their fins. Each left deep groove-like scar in the tarmac.

The bombs crashed through the walls surrounding the machine-tool workshops and shelters, and then

exploded. Fiebig swung his aeroplane around again in a wide arc and came in again, machine gunning as he flew over. It has been said by several people that he was machine-gunning workers as they ran to the shelters. Whilst possible, I have not been able to confirm this. This second run may have been to assess the bomb damage but, whatever the reason, it was dire mistake to come back.

Engaged by light ground fire the crippled Junkers was hit. It staggered for some five miles before coming to ground at East End Green Farm near Hertingfordbury, where it burned out. All the crew survived.

On the ground the damage was catastrophic, twenty-six employees had been killed and many injured, one of the bombs had exploded in one of the underground shelters. Unknown to Fiebig and his crew some of the bombs they had just released exploded right in the middle of Britain's latest twin engined fighter production line. Consequently the development and main output of the Mosquito was put back by months.

As the Junkers' machine-guns were firing the bomber was hit several times. One direct hit damaged the horizontal stabiliser. The starboard engine began to issue smoke and then burst into flames. Seconds later it stopped dead, leaving the propeller windmilling, Fiebig feathered the propeller to reduce vibration and drag and left the scene of devastation trailing a long black plume of smoke.

Numerous people witnessed the aeroplane passing over and saw the rear canopy jettisoned, followed by several steel helmets and other items being thrown out. One lady remembers the Junkers passing over and later found a cloth Luftwaffe cap from one of the crew in a local field.

Another eye-witness was 10 year old Cyril Golder who saw the burning bomber pass right over his house. There was a slight thump at the front door of their house and upon investigation Cyril saw a leather flying helmet lying on the doorstep. Some two years later Cyril was walking his pet dog over a bramble infested field known locally as the Blackberry Field, when his dog chased a rabbit into a dense patch of undergrowth. The ever investigative Cyril looked in and spotted a tube like object. Closer examination revealed a complete German MG15 machine gun with a saddle drum of bullets.

He ran off and told his father who then went to the locally billeted troops at The Woodman Pub; the gun was later extricated from the dense brambles and taken away.

The burning aeroplane gradually got lower and lower. The crew who, had decided to stay put, could see a fairly flat field ahead and Fiebig decided to make a landing there. Wrestling with the non-responsive controls he managed to lower the main undercarriage in preparation to landing, but the bomber was so low by now that it tore through the top of a thick hawthorn hedge and skidded onto the damp stubble surfaced field.

Almost immediately the port undercarriage collapsed and the Junkers slewed round violently, finally coming to rest with the starboard engine and wing fuel tank fiercely ablaze. The crew clambered from the cockpit and ran off across the fields to be finally captured about a mile away and taken under escort to Hatfield police station. After processing they were all eventually to end up in Canada for the remainder of the war. All were repatriated to Germany in 1947.

Before crashing there was time for the pilot of the bomber to feather the propeller blades in an attempt to keep airborne.

WITNESSES

D.G.Campbell:

"I believe it was during the time that the Luftwaffe was making daring daylight strikes at airfields that a Ju88 attacked de Havillands. Bombs struck the factory and tragically hit the apprentice school killing and wounding many. It made a second run, machine gunning as it went, but I believe was then hit from a Bofors gun mounted on the factory roof, manned by the LDV (Home Guard). It force landed on my cousin's farm, near Panshanger airfield, tearing off the port undercarriage leg and slewing round flat on the ground. The weather at the time was low cloud and overcast, probably making a bale out impossible. The aeroplane may have been on fire and I think the gunner was wounded. My cousin and a few others covered the crew with shotguns until the police arrived. The aeroplane was burned and a total wreck. All I have written is from memory; I had a friend who cycled all the way from

St.Albans to see the wreck. As an ex-pilot myself I consider that they did rather well….from the German point of view."

R.Mason-Jones ex-tenant of Roxford Farm

"I was working in some buildings at Waterhall Farm when the plane crashed. One of my father's men came from the fields and said a German plane had crashed. I thought he was talking nonsense as the small training planes from Hatfield, and the dummy aerodrome at Panshanger, often practised landing in the field behind the cottages. They never did more than touch down and go up again. I looked across the river and people were flocking down from Little Berkhampsted over the bridge and across the fields. I ran to the cottage to get my Home Guard rifle and two clips of ammunition. On the way I met Mr Anstey, a Sergeant in the Home Guard. The crew of the Junkers 88 had vanished and Mr Anstey organised a search. We spread out and crossed the next field intending to beat the large wood towards Hertingfordbury Station.

As we approached the wood three German airmen got out of the ditch beside the wood. One of them handed over a small pistol to an RAF Private who had joined in the search party. We all went towards my house, where Mrs Pasteur from Roxford House arrived complete with a tray of tea and cake for everyone. The police arrived having come up the road by East End Green. The crewmen were then separated and taken to separate rooms in my house. Later they were each taken away in separate vehicles.

It all happened along time ago. I think only one engine of the aircraft had been on fire when it crashed. It was quite out when I later looked at the wreckage. A squad of soldiers came and took charge. They were billeted in a nearby cottage and at night did not leave a sentry on duty at the wreck. I thought at first they did no damage at de Havilland's, but I had a friend whose brother and father were in the workshop that was bombed and were lucky to get out alive. I seem to remember the plane actually tried to land at de Havilland's once it was damaged, but was driven off by machine gun fire. There was talk that the plane came over Birch Green and machine-gunned the houses there, but this was not true."

Arthur Deamer - de Havilland employee

"I was employed as an apprentice at the de Havilland Aircraft Company in 1940, when I was seventeen years old, in what was called the D.H.94 workshop.

A Ju 88 crew in flying clothing, just like the men who landed at Hertingfordbury.

69

This department housed the D.H.94 (a small monoplane) assembly, the panel beating and sheet metal sections and a tank section where I worked. This section made tanks for the Tiger Moth, Queen Bee (a radio controlled target aircraft) Albatross, Airspeed Oxford and the D.H Rapide etc.

During 1940 we started work on repairing fuel tanks for the Hawker Hurricane aircraft that had been shot up during The Battle of Britain (how we cursed those rivets). At the beginning of the war millions of productive hours were lost by workers going to the shelters when an air raid was in progress and, due to serious loss of production, the Government (under D.O.R.A.) decreed that shelter would only be sought when imminent danger was present.

On 3 October 1940, a wet and drizzly day I believe, at 11 am approximately a voice came over the Tannoy system, which shouted 'For Christ's sake take cover'. All personnel proceeded to the indoor shelters in an unhurried manner and within a few minutes there were six large explosions. An oxygen cylinder was blasted through the wall of the shelter I was in. Fortunately no one was injured in this shelter. On leaving the shelter I was amazed to see no buildings left; all there was to see was an enormous pile of ironwork and equipment in ruins. It became immediately evident that the other indoor shelter had had a direct hit, and it was obvious there would be many casualties.

During the next few weeks I was engaged with some older men sorting out tools, jigs and other equipment for salvaging. During this time there were many grisly finds and the workers became very wary of going to the indoor shelters. Egged on by a pair of Union agitators, hundreds of employees would run out onto the aerodrome rather than go to these primitive tunnel type indoor shelters.

As far as I can recollect there were twenty-six men killed in this incident (including three supervisors who did not go to the shelters), Mr Dawson a

The crash site of the Junkers Ju 88 today, the march of time has changed it forever.

foreman, 'Gus' a chargehand and Harry Fordham also a chargehand. A number of men could not be identified and were buried in a communal grave at St. Etheldredas Church in Old Hatfield. The others were buried privately.

After this it came to light that the enemy aircraft had crash-landed in a field at Hertingfordbury. When interrogated (so the story goes) it appears the pilot circled the aerodrome several times, very low because of the weather and this pilot, who had previous connections with de Havilland Trade School, had recognised the clock tower at Jack Holdings. The aeroplane was spotted by someone in the observation post at Hatfield aerodrome, hence the urgent plea to take cover over the Tannoy (this plea was by Jock Alladyce the Works Manager). Six bombs bounced off the tarmac apron on the airfield side (the marks could be seen on the tarmac) and landed in the middle of the large workshop area.

CRASH INVESTIGATION

Immediately after the crash several local people walked across the fields to the scene, one man who was quite an eccentric ran over to the burning wreck. He began tapping on the cockpit area shouting, "Come out come out," but the crew had escaped minutes before. Some people managed to remove some items from the blazing wreck before the authorities arrived. The largest of these was a complete dinghy removed from the fuselage just behind the cockpit. A day or so later one of the swastika panels was cut from the vertical stabiliser and the two MG15 machine-guns removed from the jettisoned cockpit section.

These trophies were to remain for many years in a small private museum on the site of Hatfield aerodrome. The paint scheme of this aeroplane was standard for the time, in that the under surfaces were light blue and the upper surfaces were green and brown splinter camouflaged. This particular aeroplane had a white bar painted on the port side of the tailfin, which partially obscured the swastika marking and the Werke Nummer. Another white bar was painted on the upper surface of the port wing tip. The spinners were white and green.

66 YEARS ON

Of the de Havilland's wartime buildings a few still remained in situ in early 2005. However, the whole site has been subjected to massive development. Many original buildings are now gone forever, existing only as a piles and spreads of broken brick strewn across weed infested areas soon to be built on.

The crash site of 3Z+BB has also gone. The field's surface has been remodelled into huge earth banks and the spot where the Junkers ended its days is now under about twenty feet of landfill rubbish. Knowing that the landfill work was soon to start, I went there with a metal detector a few months before this field was torn apart by heavy plant and located a few scattered bits of 3Z+BB.

THE BISHOP'S STORTFORD 88

WEDNESDAY 16 OCTOBER 1940

Aircraft:	Crew:
Junkers Ju 88 A-5 Werke Nummer 0317	Hauptmann E. Hass
4D+DM Stab 1./KG 30	(Gruppenkommandeur) (Killed)
Location:	Feldwebel J. Kessels. (Killed)
Adjacent to Bishop's Stortford Church	Feldwebel G. Suhr. (Killed)
Time:	Kriegsberichter A. Doppelfeld
19.50 hours	(of Lw.Kr.Ber. Kp1). (Killed)

At 19.50 hours on Wednesday 16 October 1940 residents in Bishop's Stortford heard and saw a large explosion in the sky, followed by a second explosion as something smashed to earth in the vicinity of the church. The 'something' had been a Junkers Ju 88A-5 operating with Stab 1/Kampfgeschwader 30. Throughout the day Luftwaffe raids had been much reduced, in the main only solitary aeroplanes penetrated inland. Radar plotted a total of only forty enemy raiders over the UK for the entire day.

"That's a nice little souvenir." One of the partly buried engines and three propeller blades sticking out of the ground.

COMBAT

The exact cause for the massive aerial explosion and ensuing crash are unknown. No anti aircraft fire or sounds of combat attributable to the aircraft being attacked by a night fighter were heard in the vicinity. The bomber might have been damaged some considerable distance away. Some accounts do state that this aeroplane was indeed a victim of local AA fire. No bullet strikes indicating aerial combat were found in the wreckage.

WITNESSES

Many locals went to the crash site at the time. One gentleman even managed to remove a blood spattered Luftwaffe cloth eagle emblem from a tatter of uniform as a souvenir.

Remnants of parachutes were found hanging on this chestnut tree, which still stands today surrounded by houses!

CRASH INVESTIGATION

Much of the debris had been spread across Cable Field and the surrounding area bordering the old A119 road to Much Hadham. A main undercarriage leg with deflated tire, a shattered and partly buried section of engine with attached contorted blades were visible, as well as remains of some crew members in a

large Chestnut tree. This tree was festooned in shredded, partially deployed, parachute canopies. Wreckage was spread far and wide and amongst it the crash investigators managed to salvage a manufacturer's plate from the Junkers Flugzeug und Motoren Werke Dessau. The Werke Nummer of one engine was found to be 477. A large very battered external bomb rack was located, along with three twisted MG 15 machine-guns. Sometime afterwards another bomb rack was found in quite good condition.

66 YEARS ON

Examining the site some fifty years later anodised alloy was very much in evidence in the soil of the fields and beneath the large chestnut tree that still remained. Several manufacturer's plates were found, as well as a three-inch section of propeller blade. A small fragment of instrument bearing the name Lorenz was also retrieved near this tree. Other interesting finds included a round from a flare pistol. A large twisted oval disc bearing an eagle and swastika and the word Neuestadt upon it was also located. It is thought this could well have originated from the briefcase of Kriegsberichter A. Doppelfeld. Incredibly, whilst checking the perimeter hedgerow in the early 1990s, a two foot long strip of Luftwaffe issue dinghy was found still stuck in the branches of a dense section of hedge.

Since then this site has been subject to intense development and has been totally lost under a new housing estate. Amongst all these new houses there still stands a very mature Chestnut tree, the very one that had been draped in German parachutes all those years ago.

A souvenir taken at the time; a Luftwaffe eagle cut from the tunic of one of the Ju 88's crew.

THE BENDISH HEINKEL

Aircraft:	Crew:
Heinkel He 111 H-5	Leutnant Julius Tengler Pilot (Injured)
Werke Nummer 3628 1H+ET 3./KG 26	Gefreiter Wolfgang Eurl . Observer (Killed).
Location:	Gefreiter Franz Reitmayer. Flight Mechanic
West of Church Lane, Bendish.	(Injured).
Time:	Unteroffizier Hubert Faber. Radio Operator
22.12 Hours	(Injured)
	Unteroffizier Hans Zender. Radio Operator and
	Y Verfahren operator (Slightly injured)

Shot down by Squadron Leader A.T.D. Sanders and Pilot Officer Sutton of
264 Squadron in a Defiant night fighter.

As the Battle of Britain drew to a close life returned to normal. At night the irregular drone of a highflying raider would be heard as children lay in bed. Occasionally the drone of several enemy aeroplanes would be heard, such as on the night of the Coventry raid in November 1940. Once civilians were machine-gunned in the street in Stevenage, the aeroplane involved being identified as a Dornier Do 17. Men walked up country lanes to join their Home Guard comrades for a pint of bitter and a game of cards in the village hall, or found themselves secreted in woods on manoeuvres on rainy windswept nights. For the people of Hertfordshire it seemed for a while that the Phoney War had returned. This would all change on the night of 8 April at the small hamlet of Bendish.

THE NIGHT OF 8-9 APRIL 1941

On the night of the 8-9 April 1941 the priority target was Coventry. The Heinkels of 3./KG26 were scheduled to bomb the town between 22.00 and 23.00 hours. The weather conditions were perfect with clear skies and slight cloud at high altitude. Although KG26`s Heinkels were equipped with 'Y Verfahren' several crews opted for visual bombing. 237 Luftwaffe aeroplanes reached Coventry that night, resulting in a concentrated raid that released 315 tonnes of high explosive, combined with 25,000 incendiary bombs. Many important industrial targets were hit and a total of 281 persons lost their lives. A subsidiary raid was launched against Portsmouth, this being delivered by 43 aeroplanes.

COMBAT

Around 21.15 hours Julius Tengler and his crew left Le Bourget airfield in France bound for Coventry. The previous night he had been on a raid to Glasgow, but inclement weather had resulted in the raid not being successful. The Heinkel was loaded with canisters of incendiary bombs and an externally slung SC500 bomb.

As the bomber slipped over the English coast Squadron Leader A T D Sanders and his gunner, Pilot Officer Sutton, were approaching Beachy Head in their Boulton Paul Defiant. A Ground Controller using primitive 'Radar' then sent the Defiant a message, sending them towards an inbound raider flying at approximately 16,000 feet. Sanders gave chase. The pursuit continued over the London area and shortly afterwards his Defiant became 'boxed in' by very accurate AA fire. Just as Sanders sent a radio request for the gunners to cease fire he caught sight of his quarry. The target was about 500 feet in front of him. Closing in to the target Sanders identified it as an enemy raider, but could not be sure what type. The turret gunner then gave the raider a two second burst of fire with his four Browning guns. Realising that they were under attack the Heinkel crew jettisoned the large externally mounted, but the damage had already been done.

The Heinkel's fuselage and port engine had been hit by gunfire and almost immediately the engine caught fire. In the Heinkel all hell had broken loose; the aeroplane was on fire in several areas including the cockpit, one crewmember was dead and others had bullet wounds. The pilot took no evasive action. Sanders moved back into position for another attack. Positioning himself below the bomber at a range of 50 yards, Sutton fired two more lengthy bursts. Almost immediately the Heinkel was engulfed in flames, turned over and plummeted straight down.

The Heinkel's starboard engine was screaming as it entered its final dive. An eyewitness, Gerald Walker, remembers how it lit up the night sky as it fell. Both wingtips outboard of the engines were torn off and fluttered away into the night. The main wreckage continued falling with fragments being shredded from it by the violent slipstream. As it approached the ground it went into a flat spin, which broke off the tail unit. Gliding at high speed over the Bendish rooftops it slipped from sight down the valley into the park where it thumped into the ground and exploded.

The Boulton Paul Defiant night fighter with its four-gun turret was in the front-line of Britain's defences in 1941.

After a few moments incendiary bombs began burning, creating bright white areas in the conflagration. Machine-gun rounds exploded. Minutes after impact a main undercarriage tyre burst in the fierce heat, sending a shower of sparks twisting up into the sky. Later Hitchin Fire Brigade was called out to extinguish the flames, arriving about half an hour after impact.

Of the crew of five it seems that four baled out into the night sky, the fifth, Gefreiter Wolfgang Eurl, was not so fortunate. One of the bursts of fire from the Defiant had put one bullet through his head and another through his mouth. His body was found next day lying about 100 yards from the road between Breachwood Green and Lilley Bottom. The body was discovered by a passer by who spotted a partially deployed parachute canopy billowing in the wind, with the body of the young Gefreiter still attached. However, someone had found him previously as it was evident all his pockets had been turned out. This was considered by the Police to be a serious issue, but despite investigations the identity of the pocket pilferer was never established.

Many years later I heard that someone had a pair of navigational dividers and some paper money, purportedly taken from one of the crew of this Heinkel. It would seem some of the contents of Wolfgang Eurl's pockets had resurfaced after nearly half a century. How Eurl got out of the plane is in itself a mystery. Perhaps in desperate moments some of his comrades had partially deployed his chute and thrown him out, thinking that if he were unconscious he would at least have some chance of survival.

Of the remaining crew Reitmayer, the flight mechanic, had been seriously wounded in the left arm and landed on the edge of Whitehall Spinney, just to the rear of Whitehall Farm. Despite suffering from loss of blood, he managed to stumble across to the farm and surrendered himself to the soldiers billeted there. He was joined a while later by Tengler, and then they were both taken to Kings Walden Bury.

'Fly-Tipping Luftwaffe Style' the unrecognisable wreck of the Bendish Heinkel. Its tail-section fell 50 yards away from the main wreckage.

Here, some thirty minutes later, the third member of their crew, Huber Faber, joined them. Faber landed to the south west of Kings Walden Park close to Heath Farm.

Hans Zender, who was responsible for the operation of the delicate 'Y Verfahren' equipment, came down between Parsonage Farm and Whitehall Farm, close to a coppice locally known as The Nursery. He was the only crewmember to evade capture and injury. He made his way down to the Preston-Ley Green Road. Later on as he passed a cottage on the edge of Preston Hills Wood and at the junction of Dead Womans Lane he removed his headgear and threw it into the garden. It was found by the owner next morning and handed in.

Daybreak found Zender in the village of Preston. Mr W Darton was just getting ready to go to work when he heard somebody outside. Looking out from his bathroom window he was surprised to see Zender looking up at him. "What do you want to do with me?" said a tired and very dishevelled Zender. Mr Darton rushed downstairs and, after giving the airman something to eat, contacted the authorities and handed him over.

A few hours after Zender was taken in, Pilot Officer Sutton arrived at the crash site of the Heinkel. The wreckage was very hot and still smoking slightly. However, the heat did not deter Sutton from extracting a damaged MG15 machine-gun, which was later retained as a trophy by No.264 Squadron. After interrogation Tengler, Reitmayer and Faber were taken to a military hospital. Wolfgang Eurl's body was collected and taken to Hitchin for burial. His remains were not exhumed in the 1960s and he still lies there today.

The grave in Hitchin cemetery of Wolfgang Eurl, the observer of the Heinkel that crashed at Bendish.

WITNESSES

David Stedman had been attending some Home Guard training at the local parish hall that night. Instead of going straight home as usual, he decided to go to the army canteen at King's Walden with a friend to play a few games of billiards. This canteen could also be used by the Home Guard providing they were in uniform.

Eventually David decided to head home at around 22.00 hours and cycled down the lanes towards Parsonage Farm on the road to Preston. He could clearly hear the sounds of an air battle going on very high above him. Stopping he then heard and saw an aeroplane go into a screaming dive, and watched as it hit the ground. He saw that the fire was intense and its glow was visible to the southeast beyond King's Walden Park. He reached the corner at the entrance to Parsonage Farm, and turned right passing, Whitehall Farm and Frogmore in a couple of minutes.

Just beyond the gates to the park a farmer and two ATS girls met him. They told him a parachutist had landed in the park. David fixed his bayonet and cautiously went to check. It wasn't long before he found Julius Tengler lying on his back, still attached to his parachute and only just conscious. David knelt down and informed the enemy airman that everything would be OK, and Tengler

Julius Tengler, the Heinkel's pilot.

muttered something in reply. He looked to be in discomfort so David removed the throat microphones that were tangled round Tengler's neck.

Shortly afterwards some soldiers and an Air Raid Warden joined David. They had great difficulty to removing Tengler from his parachute, but finally managed to release the it and half carried their captive to a car. Tengler was then driven to Whitehall Farm, which was being used as a command post for an exercise taking place that night in King's Walden Park.

Hubert Faber later wrote an account of that night:

"As I came down through the air I could see the parachutes of my comrades and the burning aircraft below me. I landed in pasture or a field, however my parachute remained caught in a small tree and I was hanging just off the ground for a short while. I had been wounded in the left leg by a phosphorous bullet and I was injured in both hands.

I was able to free myself and hobbled to where I thought my comrades would be. Unfortunately I could not find anyone, so I decided to return to where I had left my parachute. On the way back I was taken prisoner by Home Guards (later established as armed civilians consisting of a clergyman and his son) they took me to a nearby village. In the village there were many people on the road.

One Englishman who could speak some German told me that someone was fetching a car, then I would be taken to English soldiers, and that's how it was. The guards did not bring their weapons into the car, but opened the side windows and pointed their weapons in from the running boards. So we journeyed through the darkness of the night. When I got out I was handed to some soldiers, one of these was a Pole. They brought the German speaking Pole to me. He had a great hatred of the Germans and he expressed this.

I was taken into a room where there were two of my comrades, Reitmayer and Tengler. Tengler lay rolling about on the floor, it seems he had knocked himself against the tail after he baled out and had internal injuries. Franz Reitmayer had a wounded left arm and had lost a lot of blood, he was very weak. I could not grasp why all the people in the room were so eager to get hold of souvenirs. As I took off my flying suit they came at me from all sides with scissors to cut off my shoulder epaulettes, collar tabs and all my badges.

After that, and only then, were our wounds provided for and we were taken to an ambulance and on to hospital. There I lay along time with Reitmayer in the same room. We received medical attention and were taken to separate rooms.

When I asked after my comrades I was told that they are here no more, having been taken to a special hospital.

I had many visits from an interrogation officer who was an Austrian. There were things he wanted to know. My unit was the third group of Kampfgeschwader 26, the Lion Geschwader. It was a special group with special orders. We flew on a directional beam 'Y Verfahren'. The 'Y Verfahren' system gave the pilot a series of dots and dashes in a beam, when the noise was continuous you were on target. Directly over the target it gave a signal to release the bombs.

This system was very secret. We flew in advance of other units; our bomb bays were laden with incendiary bombs to mark the target, usually with one heavy bomb as well, so that the following aircraft knew when to drop their bombs. The officer interrogated me repeated about 'Y Verfahren'. I gave plausible answers, which did not seem to satisfy him.

One day when he was with me he said the doctor would be coming to look at my wounds and it would not hurt, as I would get an injection. Afterwards, when I became fully awake and established my whereabouts, I realised that I was still wearing the old bandage. It had not been changed. I did not see this interrogating officer again during my residence in the hospital, but I was visited by the RAF pilot who had shot me down.

As my wound started to heal I was taken to the military hospital at Knutsford, near Manchester. The reception at Manchester railway station and the journey through the town centre was very un-nerving. The night before there had been an air attack on Manchester and the civilian population were still very shocked, as of course I can well understand. Today I am only too thankful that I had a uniformed escort to protect me. Behind the cordon the civilians threatened me, calls like 'Kill him' were shouted at me.

In the military hospital I was again with more German PoWs. There came new wounded prisoners from the Luftwaffe and Kriegsmarine, some from the Bismarck. They brought with them the latest national news. Reitmayer went from here to an exchange camp and was repatriated in 1943, exchanged for British prisoners.

After my convalescence I was sent to the PoW camp at Bury near Manchester; it was a former textiles factory. Here we began to get the feeling we were PoWs, the food was not too good...something we could understand as the English civilians probably had the same. The guards here were variable, the Scots had their own peculiarities.

On 22 December 1941 I, with the greater part of the camp, transferred to Canada. The journey was by train, then a freighter across the sea in convoy. The camp in Canada was very small, containing about 800 prisoners. The weather was pretty awful at times, but was made easier by the help of YMCA supplies.

I willingly went to work as a lumberjack, it made a very pleasant change. After residence in the woods as a lumberjack I was taken to another camp at Medicine Hat, Shottbridge. This was in the province of Alberta. Each camp numbered about 10,000 men. I can only say, looking back, that in Canada we had a good time until the end of the war.

In 1946 we were transported on a cargo ship back to England. There we could go to a camp in Scotland or a work camp. I declared myself ready for work and was sent to Wales. From this camp we were sent to local farms in the area of Tenby, Pembroke and Carmarthen.

At the end of 1946 I was sent to a second camp and prepared for my release. In December 1946 I began my journey home from Hull. In Germany I stayed in three camps but at last, on the 5th January 1947, I was released from imprisonment. I had been imprisoned for six years. It was not easy for me to find myself a free man again, without a home, in a destroyed Germany."

Hans Zender's health deteriorated rapidly in captivity. He died in 1947, a broken man.

CRASH INVESTIGATION

Next day at the crash scene it could be seen that the impact point was a spread of ash, clinker and once molten alloy, from this protruded the tops of the two engines with one propeller blade pointing upwards. The heat had been so fierce that even the machine guns had melted, only small parts of them were found. The engines had penetrated the ground to a depth of two feet, the fishtail exhaust stubs clearly still visible on each engine. A hundred feet away lay the battered tail unit with a tail-mounted grenade launching device installed.

Upon examination the mechanism for this was found to have been freshly greased, possibly indicating recent installation. A hook assembly was located for the assisted take of system known as Schleuderstart. The vertical stabiliser had the letters 'ET' stencilled in white on it. Manufacturers plates from the wreckage showed the manufacturer Land zu See Leichtbau, Kiel. Other component plates were dated June to September 1940. A number of .303 bullet strikes were visible, some appeared to have come from port-astern and some from ahead-upwards at an angle of 45 degrees. A large external bomb rack was also recovered.

The Heinkel had an overall paint scheme of light blue under surfaces and olive green upper surfaces. However for night operations large amounts of black distemper had been applied. This application was often very haphazard but in this case, the tail and unit makings had been quite carefully painted over. The propeller spinners were yellow, but had small amounts of distemper applied to tone them down.

65 YEARS ON

Some years ago I was researching wartime records in Hitchin Museum when I came across detailed records concerning local wartime air crashes. Mention was made of a Heinkel He 111 H-5 that had crashed somewhere near Church

Lane, Bendish. I managed to locate Church Lane, which was little more than a rough track. The records I had, stated that the wreckage had impacted to the east of this lane and then I spotted reference was made to the west! I visited some people in Bendish to see if I could determine the precise point of the crash. One very elderly gentleman could remember the glow of the fire visible from Park Gate, but he never went to investigate.

The crash site of 1H+ET was investigated in 1992. The places where the engines had impacted were found and, at a depth of two feet, part of a compacted spinner was found still bearing traces of yellow paint. Beneath this was a large section of grey painted cowling structure complete with clasps still showing red painted alignment marks. Fragments of MG 15 machine-gun, pieces of the the front gun position and some contorted fragments of Plexiglas were also recovered. The entire impact area was covered in a layer of clinker and ash containing rusted fittings, engine fragments, instruments and corroded airframe to a depth of ten inches. The whole field is very flint ridden and some of the excavated examples still bore scorch marks and fractures from the intensity of the heat. Several exploded rounds of 7.92 ammunition were found dated 1939 and 1940.

The port wing, complete with landing light and Balkankreuz painted on it, landed several hundred yards from the main crash site. It was recovered by some locals, and spent over 40 years as part of a rabbit hutch at Law Hall Farm. Eventually it was donated to Old Warden Air Museum. It was here that I managed to examine it. There were still traces of green and blue paint as well as the gritty textured black distemper that had been applied to the upper surfaces. Of particular interest were two bullet holes penetrating the under wing surfaces and exiting out through the upper. Also interesting was the patched and repaired bullet hole or flak splinter on the leading edge.

David still has Tengler's throat microphones and an elderly ex-Home Guard gentleman has one of Faber's shoulder epaulettes that was cut from his flying suit.

The Luftwaffe loss report from KG26 showing details of the Heinkel's crew.

lfo. Nr.	Ort und Tag des Verlustes	Staffel u/m.	Dienstgrad	Dorname	Familienname, Truppenteil Nr. der Erkennungsmarke	Geb tag	
1	2	3	4	5	6	7	
1	Feindflug Wahrscheinlich Quadr. 1241 15 West 23.11.Uhr 8. 4. 1941.	9. / K.G.26	Leutnant Flsgfhr.	Julius	Tengler III./ K.G. 26 51 905 / 95		
2	"	"	Gefr. Beob.	Wolf- gang	Buerl III./ K.G. 26 51 905 /97	5. 2. 22.	
3	"	"	Uffz. Funk.Bord	Hubert	Faber III./ K.G. 26 51 905 / 103		
4	"	"	Gefr. B.M.	Frans	Reitmeyer III./ K.G. 26 51 905 / 102		
5	"	"	Uffz. B.Funk.	Hans	Zender III./ K.G. 26 51 905 / 131	10. 12. 14.	
	Bemerkungen: Ursache unbekannt.						

III./ Kampfgeschwader 26

82

THE WHITWELL JUNKERS JU 88

WEDNESDAY 9 TO THURSDAY 10 APRIL 1941

Aircraft:	Crew:
Junkers Ju 88 A-1 W.Nr.4199 F1+CC 6/KG 76	Unteroffizier Heinz Kircher. Pilot. (Uninjured)
Location:	Feldwebel Fritz Stahn. Bombeschutze. (Injured)
Preston Hills Farm, nr Whitwell	Unteroffizier Hans Kellner. Bordfunker.(Injured)
Time:	Obergefreiter Willihand Vogt. Bordeschutze.
02.00 hours	(Injured)

Shot down by Sergeant Tony Staples and Sergeant Parkin of
No 151 Squadron in a Defiant night fighter.

Note: - the crew had named this aircraft 'Casa Paula' and this name was painted onto the portside section below the cockpit.

This aircraft aeroplane was a Junkers Ju 88A-1, belonging to the 6th Staffel of Kampfgeschwader 76, part of Luftflotte 3. It was coded F1+CC and bore the Werke Nummer 4199. Its overall colour scheme was blue under surfaces and olive green upper surfaces, both being covered with large areas of black distemper, there were however small areas of sandy colour scheme indicating that it had been in the North African theatre of war. This aeroplane had flown a total of sixty missions, 45 being against England and 15 against North African Targets.

This crew had taken off the day before from Creil in France, and had flown to Leuwarden in Holland to refuel and prepare for the mission. The briefed target for F1+CC was Birmingham. The incoming flight at 19,000 feet was uneventful, but just as they crossed the coast some light inaccurate AA fire was noted. The pilot descended to an altitude of 10,000 feet. As they approached Birmingham the AA fire was neither light nor inaccurate and the aeroplane suffered minor shell splinter damage.

COMBAT

Consulting the target map the crew found they were flying over a rubber factory and large warehouse. They were then attacked by a night fighter which, for some reason, they believed to be a Beaufighter. The night fighter in question was in fact a Boulton Paul Defiant that had taken off from RAF Wittering. The pilot was Sergeant Tony Staples and the gunner was Sergeant Parkin of No.151 Squadron. As it was known that Birmingham was already under attack, Staples decided to scout around the area, hoping to intercept one of the raiders. They had been airborne for about 45 minutes when Staples spotted a small light out to starboard. Closing into the light it could be seen to be from the exhaust of an aeroplane flying towards Birmingham. Coming close to the portside of the aeroplane they carried out an identification, concluded it was a Dornier 17, and opened fire. Flashes appeared all over the port wings and side of the fuselage.

Inside the Junkers Willihand Vogt thought for a split second how it sounded like stones hitting a corrugated iron rooftop. This first burst of fire seriously damaged the bomber, severely damaging the port wing and engine. The Junkers 88 immediately jettisoned its bomb load of twenty SC50 type bombs and then went into an steep dive.

The Defiant pilot turned steeply to the right and attempted to follow his target down. Still with target in view Parkin repeatedly fired short bursts but was unable to score any strikes on the bomber. Eventually the Junkers was lost to sight. Sergeant Staples now found himself below the balloon barrage and, not seeing any further intruders, decided to return to base.

Unknown to Defiant crew, Heinz Kircher managed to regain control, albeit shakily. The very badly damaged port engine started to emit showers of sparks and then streaks of flame and then stopped. Unable to feather the blades the aeroplane was now vibrating severely. The wind shrieked through several damaged panes of Plexiglas and maps and small items blew all around the cockpit interior.

After some twenty minutes flying the problems worsened. The entire port wing was ablaze and the crew took the decision to bail out. By this time their altitude had dropped to 5,000 feet and was falling. The first man out was Willihand Vogt, it had been his responsibility to open the rear escape canopy, and the remainder of the crew followed him. As soon as the crew vacated their stricken aeroplane it nose-dived and went straight down.

Preparing for a raid... Bombing up a Junkers Ju 88.

'Floodlit Friend' a
Defiant prepares for
take-off.

At 02.30 hours on 10 April it smashed into a slightly sloping field at Preston Hills Farm on the edge of Hernsfield Wood. In the night sky there was a huge flash and a glow illuminated the edges of all the surrounding woods. Like a distant peal of thunder the explosion caused all the pheasants in the nearby woods to call out in alarm for minutes afterwards.

The impact had been violent. The two engines smashed straight through three feet of thick clay and flints to embed themselves a further eight feet in the solid chalk below. The starboard engine had been at full power and so violent was its impact that the spinning propeller blades shattered and fragmented into contorted sections.

A few minutes after this Vogt landed in a large willow tree bordering a small stream near the village of Harlington. As his canopy snagged the branches it slammed him into the main trunk, painfully damaging his kneecap. He also had a backache, which was later attributed to having damaged his kidneys when his parachute opened. Eventually he released himself and wandered around the by the edge of the stream for some hours, and then decided to go into the village.

At 07.15 hours he managed to flag down a passing car driven by Mr Joe West with Mr Jack Peppiatt as passenger. Both men were on their way to work at Vauxhall's plant in Luton. Upon spotting Vogt they both thought he was an airman from the nearby Barton airfield. Seeing that he was armed it is reputed that Joe West, being a well-built rugger player, leapt from the car and knocked Vogt to the ground. He had seen Vogt struggling to release his side arm and took action; Vogt was later to say he was only offering his gun in surrender. From here the two men took Vogt to the Police House at Harlington. Once here, Police Constable Goodhall gave him a breakfast of bacon and eggs and informed the authorities.

After a lengthy period of hospitalisation and interrogations Vogt was sent by train under armed guard to Leicester. On the way some RAF personnel gave him a little money, some chocolate and a few cigarettes. From Leicester he was sent to the camp at Bury, here he met up with the rest of his crew. In December 1941 many of the inmates at Bury were transferred by freighter from Liverpool to Canada. He was kept at Ontario for most of his internment and volunteered for woodcutting with a team of French Canadians and Indians. It was another six years before he saw his homeland again.

David Stedman states that Unteroffizier Heinz Kircher came down in some trees at the southernmost corner of King'sWalden Bury park (a popular area for German airman it would seem as Tengler and Faber from the Heinkel at Bendish had landed here some 28 hours before). Releasing himself form his harness Kircher then walked up the road to Whitwell. In doing so he passed a cottage whose occupiers had been awoken by the noise of the crashing aeroplane. They saw him approaching but were later to say that they were glad that he passed them by, as he was shouting very loudly. Later Kircher returned to the cottage where one of the occupants, now armed with a shotgun, watched with relief as Kircher walked past. Kircher went along the Lilley Bottom road away from Whitwell. It was along this section of road that he was taken prisoner by Colonel Harrison, who just happened to be driving by. Colonel Harrison was later to say that he thought Kircher was, 'loud and arrogant'.

'Floodlit Foe' this time it's the enemy, a Ju 88 prepares to take off for a nocturnal raid.

Of the others, Stahn was captured near Streatley Village, whilst Kellner was captured in the village of Harlington. Kellner, having walked into the village, met Special Sergeant Adams, threw up his arms and said, Kamerad. Then, in very broken English, he proceeded to explain to Sergeant Adams that he had come down about half a mile away and that he had injured his ankle. He also made a great point of emphasising that he had thrown his pistol away.

Upon their capture a number of documents and identification items were taken from of the crew. Hans Kellner handed over his identity disc and his Ausweis. This was the standard light blue in colour and had been issued at Lechfeld on 07/02/40 the same date as that belonging to Heinz Kircher. Fritz Stahn's Ausweis had been issued in Paris on 21/02/41, and Vogt's was issued on 07/04/41.

From their interrogation it was established that they had taken off from Châteaudun and that the briefed target for that night was Birmingham. Other than these basic details the men said little under interrogation. What their interrogators were unaware of was that this crew had attended a series of in depth lectures on procedures and what to say in the event of being captured only a few days before. Had they not they attended these lectures they may have been somewhat more forthcoming.

CRASH INVESTIGATION

Mr F H Maybrick, upon whose land the Junkers had crashed, decided to go and see what all the fuss was about. Crossing his fields he came to a large smoking area of disturbed soil, from this protruded some large sections of twisted metal. Next to all this mess was a young Police Constable standing on guard. A team of RAF crash investigators appeared on the scene and Mr Maybrick confirmed to them it did not look like anyone had been on board when the aeroplane crashed. The RAF officer in charge of salvage later commented that it was an 'ordinary, run of the mill, Junkers' and that it was not a specially equipped pathfinder type. Some of the electrical equipment recovered was in reasonable condition and it was noted that the firm of Phillips in Holland had manufactured much of it. Two manufacturers plates found in the debris were from Nord Deutsche Dornier Werke, the date on them being July 1940. At this time the wreckage was so badly smashed that no unit identification markings could be ascertained. If that was the case they stood little chance of finding the hand painted words on the fuselage just below the cockpit. These were 'Casa Paula' named after a girlfriend of one of the crew.

What was ascertained, however, was the cause of the crash; numerous .303 bullet strikes could be seen on the wreckage. As to the engines, it was reported that no details were available as they were deeply buried, indeed they were to remain so for nearly half a century. The remainder of the wreckage that was salvaged was transported to a scrap yard in Oxford. A few days later, Vogt's

snagged parachute was retrieved from the tree with great difficulty by two members of the Home Guard, Mr J L Hall and Mr W Brown. It was not until a few weeks later that the rear canopy from the cockpit was located in an area of woodland near Shefford, still with a rather bent MG 15 machine gun attached.

As the sun sets a Defiant takes off to intercept enemy raiders.

WITNESSES

Thirty-five years later Willihand Vogt returned to the village of Harlington. Here he met Joe West and Jack Peppiatt, the two men who had captured him all those years before. They returned to the exact spot on the road where the capture had taken place, and a firm friendship between all three was developed. In 1992 an aviation archaeologist by the name of Peter Stanley arranged another reunion for Willihand Vogt or 'Hadi' as he prefers to be called. Ex Sergeant Tony Staples had never known that his gunner, Sergeant Parkin, had indeed shot down that raider they chased over Birmingham fifty-one years before. Through diligent research Peter Stanley finally got the Defiant crew credited with the 'kill'. Finally Tony Staples and Willihand Vogt would met. This reunion took place at the RAF Museum, Hendon. Tony Staples had just been admiring the pristine example of a Boulton Paul Defiant when Willihand Vogt came over. They shook hands and embraced. Despite the background noise and murmurs from onlookers, one of them just audibly spoke the words, 'Brothers of the air'.

After a brief conversation the two were escorted outside, where Peter had made a display of a propeller boss and reduction gear from Hadi's *'Casa Paula'*. Hadi explained that, ironically, he owed his life to Tony Staples, as after he had been shot down his Staffel had been sent to the Eastern Front, from which there were no survivors. Later it was decided to take them both to Harlington and the crash site at Preston Hills Farm. Incredibly the very tree that Hadi had got caught up in was still standing and he had several photographs taken beneath it. The small group trudged along the side of a stubble field to the spot where F1+CC had ended her days. Tony Staples and Willihand Vogt walked over the spot, gently moving tufts of stubble looking for twisted pieces of alloy. Moving aside some weeds a corroded spanner was discovered. This was picked up and within a few seconds placed back into the hands of Willihand Vogt; it had once belonged to his personal tool kit on board F1+CC.

65 YEARS ON

The crash site of this Junkers 88 has been subjected to two excavations, one in 1991 and another in 1993. The first excavation revealed both engines, fragmentary propeller blades, cockpit instruments and tons of twisted, compressed airframe. The engines were in surprisingly good condition, the fire damage and bullet strike marks could still clearly be seen on the port engine. Many manufacturer's plates were discovered dated 1940 and 1941. The second excavation in 1993 revealed more areas of compressed airframe. Today the crash site scene has changed very little, the pheasants in surrounding woodlands still give their alarm calls, but ever since that night in April 1941 they give their alert only for prowling foxes.

THE ACE AT ASHWELL

21 TO 22 JULY 1941

Aircraft:
Junkers Ju 88 C-4 R4+BL 3./NJG 2
Location:
High ground, near Ashwell
Time:
01.30 hours

Crew:
Leutnant Heinz Volker. (Pilot) (Killed)
Unteroffizier Herbert Indenbirken.
(Bordfunker) (Killed)
Feldwebel Andreas Wurstl. (Bordschutze)
(Killed)

Crashed as a result of aerial collision with Wellington R1334. This was the seventh and final enemy aeroplane to crash in Hertfordshire during World War Two.

On the night of 21-22 July, 1941, Heinz Volker and his crew were scheduled for operations again. After a shorter than usual briefing the three men walked across the drizzle swept runway of Gilze Rijen airfield in Holland. As Volker, Indenbirken and Wurstl climbed aboard their black painted Junkers night fighter the pungent aroma of dope, oil and feint traces of burned cordite greeted them.

Volker and his crew had been flying intruder missions in search of unwary British aircraft for some time, lurking in the vicinity of RAF aerodromes looking for unlucky or inexperienced victims. Increasing RAF activity near Bassingbourn had been noticed by crews of NJG 2.

One eyewitness remembered a 'Jerry' flying around Ashwell village, its engines sounding different to the RAF planes. This particular aircraft circled Ashwell, dropping flares all over the district, but after 22 July these nocturnal visits ceased. One can only surmise that Volker and his crew had been the visitor as these flare dropping missions stopped suddenly.

Operating in the same area on 10 April 1941 had been Volker's colleague, Oberleutnant Schulz, who shot down Wellington L4253. This Wellington dived vertically down and crashed into a house at

A tragic reminder of the human price of war; a crumpled German 'wound badge' picked up years later.

Ashwell. Fortunately the house was unoccupied at the time. Other night fighter victories are listed below, but have not been attributed to specific crews:

24 April 1941 a Wellington of 11 OTU based at Bassingbourn was shot down while attempting to land. It crashed into stationary Wellington R1404.

18 July 1941 Wellington X3169 was fired upon as it was about to land at Steeple Morden aerodrome and was seriously damaged.

19 August 1941 Wellington 3005 was shot down north east of Barrington.

Volker crossed the 'enemy' coast just below The Wash, skirted the Norfolk Coast, and then turned inland passing near Newmarket. Despite having been tracked by the Observer Corps for some considerable time, little action was taken by the defences. Just south of Newmarket a single searchlight flicked on, the erratic beam wavering into the night sky, however after a few moments it was turned off.

A Junkers Ju 88C nightfighter of the type flown by Heinz Volker.

By now Volker and his crew had dropped to around 700 feet. The Junkers 88 was now streaking over the flat-fielded edges of the Fenland, on its course to the Bassingbourn area. As undulating hill tops with small copses or single trees appeared Volker commenced a very wide circular flight path across the

airfield in the hope of catching any returning British bombers or, preferably, inexperienced training flights.

In the early stages of the war Volker's crew had gained a prestigious reputation. Operating over various areas of England they had so far managed to shoot down a total of seven British aeroplanes:

28/10/40 – a Hampden near Scampton.
22/12/40 – a Blenheim near Cranwell.
04/04/41 – a Wellington near West Raynham.
17/04/41 – a Hampden near Finningley.
24-25/4/41 – three Blenheims near Lindholme.

COMBAT

At about 01.25 hours, having been circling for some minutes, Wurstl suddenly shouted out. They had passed something, he was sure of it. A huge shape had floated by and for a second he was sure he had seen at least one yellow-blue flamed exhaust. Wurstl was indeed correct, he had just had a fleeting glimpse of Wellington R1334, packed with trainees from 11 OTU. The crew on board R1334 that night were:

The Vickers Wellington, mainstay of Bomber Command in 1941.

Sergeant C A MacAllister, Wireless Operator
Flight Sergeant W A Stewart, Pilot
Sergeant S Stewart, Wireless Operator
Sergeant R E Hibbert, Wireless Operator
Sergeant F S Houston, Pilot
Sergeant T Manning, Gunner

Leutnant Heinz Volker, 'the Ace at Ashwell'.

Sergeant B C Thompson, Pilot
Sergeant C M S Lewis, Observer

Volker swung the Junkers around in a very tight turn and all the crew scanned the night sky. Many hundreds of feet ahead a tiny pinprick of light was spotted, getting larger and larger. Then in the darkness the form of a huge aeroplane could be seen. Heinz Volker had seen it too. He throttled back, allowing the British aeroplane to slide ahead. Realigning his aeroplane, Volker positioned himself right behind his unwary victim. Just as Volker opened fire the Wellington pilot began some violent evasive action as tracer shells skimmed past. Volker followed and fired a three second burst at the target. The crew of the Junkers 88 could see the bright flashes of strikes as the cannon shells exploded on, in and through the wings and fuselage of the Wellington. The Wellington immediately caught fire, trailing a great banner of fuel-fed flame from one wing. Small sparks and pieces of fabric and airframe came away from the doomed Wellington and tumbled back past their attacker, but still the pilot tried further evasive manoeuvres.

Volker watched the Wellington go into a tight turn to port. The flames from the Wellington created a flickering orange glow in the cockpit of the Junkers. Volker realised that he was too close and attempted to out-turn the falling Wellington. However, at his speed that was simply not possible. Like a moth to a light, Volker had been briefly mesmerised by the glow from his victim, drawing him and his crew in too close.

At 600 feet above Ashwell both aircraft exploded in one terrific blinding white flash that illuminated the countryside for miles around. The burning wreckage fell to earth. The cockpit area of the Junkers 88 had disintegrated and at least one body fell out from the main wreckage to land several hundred feet away. The tail section snapped off the Junkers and landed intact in the village. The remainder belly-panned on the top of a rise in the land, exploded and then continued to burn.

The Wellington fell away from the collision fiercely ablaze and dived into an adjacent field, killing all on board. The crackle of exploding ammunition could be heard from both crashes. This was Volker's eighth and final victory.

CRASH INVESTIGATION

In the twilight hours a Wellington crew board their bomber for another sortie.

The wreckage of the German aeroplane was of great interest to the investigating authorities. Much of it had been burned out and no unit identification codes could be seen. It was established that the airframe had been manufactured by Junkers Flugzeug und Motoren Werke at Dessau. Dates on various manufacturer's plates were mainly from 1941, although one was dated September 1940. The engines were Junkers Jumo 211Gs. Three MG 17 machine guns were located, along with a single 20mm cannon.

Shortly afterwards a second 20mm cannon was found housed in a detachable pod assembly that appeared to have been part of the front of the lower gondola. The cocking bottle and firing mechanism for this gun was also found. The forward armour was a large circular bulkhead through which the three MG17s and single cannon protruded.

It was noted that the pilot's windscreen was made of especially thick glass. Only about ten feet of one wingtip remained undamaged by fire. Near to this were five unexploded SC50 bombs, all having been fitted with No.25 type fuzes. A canvas satchel marked with British roundels and containing seven types of recognition flares was found.

At the end of the first day of investigation one of the recovery crew picked up a small piece of cloth that was blowing about. This caused some excitement as it bore the embroidered name Oberfahnrich Heinz Volker. It was thus established that the 'Experte' of NJG 2 had met his death over this bleak Hertfordshire hillside. The body and other fragmentary remains of the German crew were gathered up and buried in Bassingbourn cum Kneesworth cemetery, but were later moved to Cannock Chase. Months later, when the field came to be harvested, a third 20mm cannon was found. This German night fighter had been armed with a total of three MG17s and three 20mm cannon.

The original wooden grave markers at Bassingbourn cum Kneesworth cemetery in the 1960s. Later the bodies were moved to Cannock Chase.

65 YEARS ON

Numerous individuals have examined the crash site over the last sixty-five or so years, some have made interesting discoveries in the plough soil. Lying on the surface are numerous globules of once molten aluminium, broken electrical components and exploded MG17 shell cases. The wreckage penetrated to a depth of about three feet. Dutch coins have been found over the years, the zip from a leather flying jacket and a crumpled bronze German wound badge.

MINES, BOMBS, DOODLEBUGS AND ROCKETS

A brief account of the German offensive weapons that were dropped or fell in Hertfordshire during the years 1940-45

During World War Two the first enemy high explosive bombs to fall in Hertfordshire were dropped over London Colney in June of 1940. From this point onwards a whole host of bombs were dropped over Hertfordshire by the Luftwaffe, the largest being the Parachute Mine. These were actually Naval mines that the Germans had converted for land dropping; it was an indiscriminate weapon, floating down suspended via silk cords from a huge parachute canopy.

Due to the volume of high explosive used and the fact that they exploded above ground, the surface blast from these mines could be devastating. One such mine fell near Tamworth Road in Hertford, killing three people and injuring over sixty. In this one incident the blast demolished seventeen houses, with sixty four suffering structural damage to varying degrees.

Later, on 10 October 1940, three high explosive bombs fell in the Hockerill district near Bishops Stortford. Two bombs caused no damage, but the third fell on the accommodation area (Menet House) in the college grounds killing three girl students and burying eight others in the rubble.

Most types of German bomb, from high explosive, incendiary to oil varieties fell on Hertfordshire in the years 1940-41, after this period only sporadic bombs from single intruders fell until 1944 when the German 'V' weapon offensive began using the jet propelled V-1 - known by a variety of names such as Fly Bomb, Doodlebug or Fire Arse. This pilotless, 25 feet long 'missile' had a warhead that contained 850kg of high explosive, from which the surface blast damage could be devastating.

At first the V-1s were fired from ramps in the Pas de Calais, but as the launch sites were over-run following the D Day offensive the Germans adapted Heinkel He 111 bombers to carry V-1s underneath them. Combined with the aircraft's 200 mile range (with bomb) and the range of the V-1 this meant that towns in the midlands and further a field now experienced the Doodlebug. Most eye-witnesses to the V-1 describe its sound as similar to a throbbing motorcycle with no baffles.

V-1s were followed on 8 September 1944 by an even more serious threat from the V-2, the worlds very first ballistic missile. The Germans designated this missile as the A4, having an overall height of 46 feet and weighing at 13.6 tons including one ton of high explosive in the warhead. Nothing could counter these missiles directly; from their launch they attained a speed

The drawing of the V-1 issued to the Royal Observer Corps.

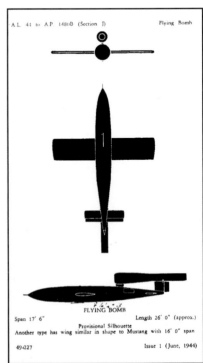

A.L. 41 to A.P. 1480B (Section J)   Flying Bomb

FLYING BOMB

Span 17' 6"   Length 26' 0" (approx.)
Provisional Silhouette
Another type has wing similar in shape to Mustang with 16' 0" span

49.227   Issue 1 (June, 1944)

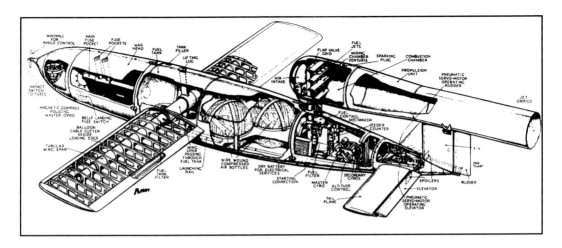

The image shows a technical cutaway drawing of the V-1 flying bomb with the following labels: WINDMILL FOR RANGE CONTROL, MAIN FUSE POCKET, FUSE POCKETS, WAR HEAD, FUEL TANK, TANK FILLER, LIFTING LUG, FLAP VALVE GRID, FUEL JETS, MIXING CHAMBER VENTURIS, SPARKING PLUG, COMBUSTION CHAMBER, PROPULSION UNIT, PNEUMATIC SERVO-MOTOR OPERATING RUDDER, JET ORIFICE, IMPACT SWITCH TO FUSES, MAGNETIC COMPASS POLICING MASTER GYRO, BELLY LANDING FUSE SWITCH, BALLOON CABLE CUTTER INSIDE LEADING EDGE, TUBULAR WING SPAR, WING SPAR PASSING THROUGH FUEL TANK, FUEL TANK FILTER, LAUNCHING RAIL, WIRE WOUND COMPRESSED AIR BOTTLES, DRY BATTERY FOR ELECTRICAL SERVICES, STARTING CONNECTION, FUEL FILTER, MASTER GYRO, SECONDARY GYROS, ALTITUDE CONTROL, TAIL PLANE, SPOILERS, ELEVATOR, PNEUMATIC SERVO-MOTOR OPERATING ELEVATOR, RUDDER, AIR INTAKE, FUEL CONTROL MECHANISM, FEEDER COUNTER

A wartime technical drawing of the V-1 as revealed to the public.

of some 3,600mph and reached an altitude of some 50 to 60 miles into the stratosphere.

Many of these were fired from Holland and would impact on the British mainland within four minutes, incredibly people went up to the hilly areas around Ashwell in 1944, where on clear evenings you could see V-2s being fired from Holland. "They looked like a tiny flickering spark, then up, up, up until out of sight." said one eyewitness.

Nuthampstead airbase was to receive a very near miss on its bomb dump when a V-2 rocket exploded there on 14 December 1944. No one was injured in this incident, but several large panels were blown off a T2 hangar near the Woodman Pub. Unusually this Nuthampstead example created a double crater, both being about ten feet deep. Another V-2 landed at Quickswood near Clothall on 4 January 1945. The blast from this rocket exploding broke windows as far away as Letchworth.

Today it is possible to see evidence of this impact as a huge section of hedge is still missing and there is a shallow crater on the hillside littered with fragments of airframe skinning and oxygen bottles from the rocket.

On 8 January 1945 the 488th V-2 landed on British soil, coming to earth at Datchworth. The last alert in Hertfordshire came on 29 March 1945 and involved the very last V-1 to fall on Britain, this also fell at Datchworth.

During the years of the Second World War a total of 258 people in Hertfordshire were killed and 689 seriously injured by German bombs, and rockets. A total of 107 V-1s and 47 V-2 rockets, 85 parachute mines and 4,358 high explosive bombs fell in Hertfordshire. This does not take into consideration the thousands of incendiary and anti personnel 'Butterfly Bombs' that the Luftwaffe dropped, nor unexploded AA shells that fell back to earth.

In the vicinity of Hertford town alone a total of 457 incendiary bombs were dropped, all posing risk to the public, their property and of course to those who had to remove and defuse them.

Many of the Luftwaffe's bombs still lie in the Hertfordshire countryside, deeply buried in the native chalk and clays. Most will never be discovered, but just occasionally a new housing or road development will reveal these poignant reminders of more hectic times. In 1998 a 1,000lb German bomb was defused in a Hertfordshire field, more recently in 2004 during the Baldock by-pass construction, two small German incendiary bombs were discovered and later removed by Bomb Disposal.

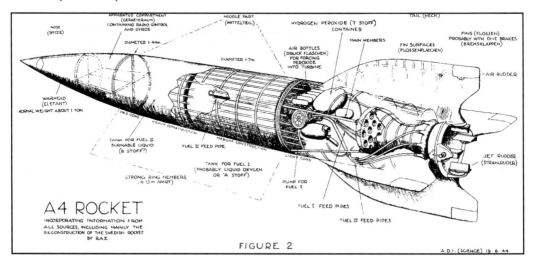

FIGURE 2

British scientists were quick to learn the secrets of the V-2 (A4) rocket as this drawing from August 1944 shows.

An American serviceman stands in the crater made by a V-2 rocket that fell on Nuthampstead. (Courtesy of Russ Abbey of Nuthampstead Airfield Research Society)

World War Two – USAAF

With the entry of the United States into the war air activity increased to a never before seen level. New aircraft made their appearance, such as the P-51 Mustang, P-38 Lightning, P-47 Thunderbolt, B-24 Liberator and perhaps most famous of all the B-17 Flying Fortress. 1944 was the peak year, for with the build up of armed forces prior to the Allied invasion of Europe, daylight raids by the USAAF intensified. Raids deep into the heart of the Reich, Occupied Europe and later French coastal targets were all undertaken. Many raids involved 'stacking up' over Hertfordshire as the bombers began to formate and head off for their target. It was not uncommon at this stage of the war for some Observer Corps stations to plot over 500 aircraft in the sky at one time.

For many people living in the area the noise of these huge armadas of aircraft would be unforgettable. Those residents living near to Nuthampstead or near the huge USAAF base Bassingbourn, just over the Hertfordshire border in Cambridgeshire, would be treated to a daily chorus of four engined heavies flying over. Locals became quite used to it, but what they never got used to was looking skywards and seeing them return, with feathered props, engines on fire, sections shot away, crossing their fingers and hoping that the smoke streaming straggler at the back would land safely.

A B-17 of the 398th Bomb Group climbs to operational altitude.

Tragically this increase in activity brought with it an increase in incidents, ranging from crash-landings to catastrophic and dramatic aerial collisions. On Saturday 12 August 1944 a B-17 named 'Tomahawk Warrior' from the 398th BG collided with a B-24H Liberator over Cheshunt, killing both crews. Just two weeks later another similar tragedy occurred involving the collision of two B-17s over the small village of Weston.

THE DESTRUCTION OF 'TOMAHAWK WARRIOR'

Aircraft involved:	**Crew:**
B17G Flying Fortress 'Tomahawk Warrior'	Pilot. Charles J Searl…Killed
Serial Number 42-102936	Co-Pilot. Albert L. Lion…Killed
398th Bombardment Group (Heavy)	Navigator. Saul J.Kempner…Killed
Based at Nuthampstead, Hertfordshire	Bombardier. Leo C. Walsh…Killed
Location:	Radio Operator. Cecil E.Kennedy …Killed
wreckage spread over wide area at	Eng/ Top Turret Gunner. James A.Beaty…Killed
Lude Farm, Penn, in Buckinghamshire	Waist Gunner. Albert W. Knight… Killed
Time:	Ball Turret Gunner. Alfred W. Bueffel…Killed
07.20 Hours	Tail Gunner. Orville M. Wilson…Killed

Second Aircraft involved:	**Crew:**
B24H Liberator	Pilot. 2nd Lt John D. Ellis…Killed
Serial Number 42-95023 DC-V+	Co-Pilot. F/O. Samuel C. Stalsby…Killed
392nd Bombardment Group (Heavy)	Navigator / Bombardier. 2nd Lt Robert B.
577th Squadron	Cox…Killed
Based at Wendling in Norfolk	Nose Gunner. S/Sgt. Clare W. Hultengren
Location:	Radio Operator. T/Sgt John H. Holling…Killed
In field between Cheshunt and Waltham Cross	Engineer. T/Sgt Stanley F. Jankowski…Killed
Time:	Top Turret Gunner. S/Sgt Jack O. Shaffer Killed
07.20 Hours	Waist Gunner. S/Sgt Frank Jr Minick…Killed
	Ball Turret Gunner. Sgt Jay V. Cable…Killed
	Tail Gunner. S/Sgt William C. McGinley…Killed.

From 06.00 hours on Saturday morning, 12 August 1944, several B-17s took off from the Nuthampstead runway to participate in a raid on the Versailles area in Occupied France. One of them was named 'Tomahawk Warrior' the pilot, Charles Searl, had named her so after the small town where he, his wife and eighteen month old daughter lived. He was the only crew member of this aeroplane to be married. The other members of the crew ranged in age from 20 to 27 and came from as far afield as Wisconsin, Michigan and Virginia.

'Tomahawk Warrior' had flown many missions, on 19 May the crew had been to Berlin, they had even completed one trip to support D-Day operations and attacked Caen and Courseulles. June 1944 saw the total number of her missions so far rise sixteen.

In July Charles Searl heard the marvellous news that he was a father again, of a little girl, sadly fate would determine that he would never live to see her. At 06.18 hours Tomahawk Warrior took off and climbed to stack up with other units over Hertfordshire.

The weather that morning was appalling, a grey mist had set in with drizzle creating very poor visibility and keeping formation was incredibly difficult. Suddenly a giant dark shape loomed out of the mist, huge rounded tailfins just yards ahead - a B-24 Liberator!

Then the two aircraft collided. For both crews all that could be heard was the uneven roar of engines, the clatter of torn panelling and rush of air through the damaged airframes.

The Liberator had taken off from Wendling in Norfolk, part of the 392nd BG force on a raid to the French airfield of Juvincourt. The huge twin-tailed bomber spiralled downwards out of control. There was nothing that could be done, and as the bomber began to disintegrate centrifugal forces trapped the crew inside. Screaming engines caused those on the ground to look up into the cloudy, moisture laden, skies above. A huge explosion was heard as the Liberator thumped down into a field just outside Cheshunt, and exploded. Wreckage and crew were scattered all over the area.

As for *Tomahawk Warrior* the initial damage, although serious, did not seem to be life-threatening. As the B-17 headed southeast at 07.00 hours several eyewitnesses saw one of its engines on fire. As she swung around over High Wycombe a second engine burst into flames.

It has always been accepted locally that Charles Searl could see that he was over a heavily populated area, and realising that the B-17 was now in a critical he struggled away from the area. It is noteworthy that not one member of the crew bailed out. An impact in the highly populated area would have been catastrophic.

B-24s of the 392nd Bomb Group.

The stricken bomber now raced low over the countryside approaching the Buckinghamshire village of Penn. Huge gouts of orange flame shot from the engines and a great streak of swirling black smoke trailed behind her. Just ahead lay Lude Farm. The flame blackened and severly damaged B17 now clattered over the farmhouse, missing it by inches, and crashed into a field just opposite.

Immediately there was a massive explosion that rocked the village of Penn. *Tomahawk Warrior*' and her crew perished in a huge fireball. One body was located in a nearby lane and two more at the edge of the field. The remainder of the crew could only be identified by information on their dog tags.

General Doolittle, who was at the HQ in High Wycombe, came to visit the crash site later in the day. The official records at Nuthampstead recorded, "Take-off 06.18 hours, 07.20 no return" a somewhat short epitaph for an incident costing 19 lives.

The nine aircrew were originally buried in Madingley, however after the war eight of them were re-interred in Arlington Cemetery in the USA.

In Cheshunt it is still widely believed that John Ellis, the pilot of the B-24 Liberator, also deliberately flew his crippled aeroplane away from the populated area of Cheshunt. In gratitude for this action the townsfolk erected a memorial plaque on the wall of one of the buildings at the American cemetery

A B-24 Liberator of the 392nd Bomb Group at Wendling.

in Madingley. An identical plaque can be found in Cheshunt Library, stating "To these gallant American airmen who on August 12th 1944 sacrificed their lives to prevent their aircraft from crashing on our homes. The residents of Cheshunt and Waltham Cross in the County of Hertfordshire dedicate this plaque in grateful memory."

Below this the names of the ten crew members are engraved. Three of these men, including pilot John Ellis, are still buried in the cemetery at Madingley in Cambridge, the remainder were returned to two different cemeteries in the USA (Zachary Taylor National Cemetery and Fort Snelling National Cemetery).

SINCE 1944

The one crew member from the B-17 still buried in the UK is Albert Knight, a waist gunner, whose grave can be found at Madingley cemetery in Cambridgeshire. On each Armistice Day at Penn Church the crew's names are read, along with men from the village who gave their lives on active service. Little American flags flutter along the path by the church door, each one bearing the name of a crew member.

Today the field where the B-17 crashed and exploded with such force has not changed greatly. In winter it is still possible to walk around the hedgerows and spot the occasional partially moss covered crumbling piece of contorted metal, all that now remains of a once battle-worthy Flying Fortress.

TWO B-17S COLLIDE OVER THE VILLAGE OF WESTON

(This chapter is dedicated to the memory of Frank Hawkes who witnessed the event and became a very good friend of the author.)

Aircraft involved:
B-17G Flying Fortress
Serial Number 42-102936
390th Bombardment Group (Heavy)
Based at Parham / Framlingham in Suffolk
Location:
wreckage spread over 1.5km in Weston Park
Time:
09.05 Hours

Crew:
Pilot. 2nd Lt Paul H Bellamy…Killed
Co-Pilot. 2nd Lt James J.Graba…Killed
Navigator. 2nd Lt Raymond A Klausing…
Survived
Bombardier. 1st Lt Joseph Y Lee…Killed
Radio Operator. Sgt Irwin W Casey…Killed
Eng/Top Turret Gunner. S/Sgt Frederick O
Walsh…Survived
Waist Gunner. Sgt Lotus R Conser… Survived
Ball Turret Gunner. Sgt Robert Hunter…Killed
Tail Gunner. Sgt Richard A McAteer…Survived.

Second Aircraft involved:
B-17G Flying Fortress 'Ding Dong Daddy'
Serial Number 42-97182
390th Bombardment Group (Heavy)
Based at Parham/Framlingham in Suffolk
Location:
In Warrens Spring Wood at Weston
Time:
09.05 Hours

Crew:
Pilot. 1st Lt George E Smith …Killed
Co-Pilot. 2nd Lt Carleton Sacco…Killed
Navigator. 2nd Lt Robert G Taylor…Killed
Bombardier. 2nd Lt Herman R Collins…Killed
Radio Operator. T/Sgt Victor G Graff…Killed
Eng / Top Turret Gunner. T/Sgt Allen J
McCasland Jr…Killed
Waist Gunner. S/Sgt Martin I Kilbride…Killed
Ball Turret Gunner. S/Sgt Michael K Kasarda…Killed
Tail Gunner. Corporal Gus G Brubaker…Killed.

At approximately 09.00 hours on Saturday 26 August 1944 the villagers of Weston heard the now familiar droning hum of bombers massing for a raid. So familiar had this sound become that rarely did they cast an eye upwards these days. Today would be different and for miles around everyone would stare up at the sky in horror.

A few minutes before young Frank Hawkes had stood watching a Tiger Moth perform some aerobatics over his village, but the noise from its tiny engine had been drowned out by the approaching bombers. A dull boom was heard and a high pitched, screaming, whine as the pitch of engines dramatically changed. "Sommits up with the Yanks" friend Alf said to Frank, as they both

Opposite page;
2nd Lt Paul H Bellamy
the pilot of B-17
42- 102936 which
collided with the B17
named 'Ding Dong
Daddy'. (Courtesy of M
and J Huffman)

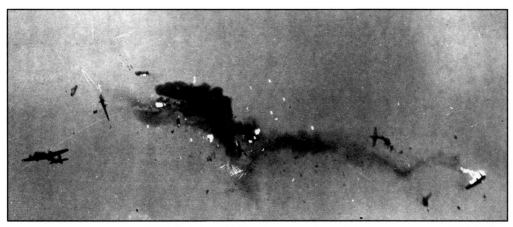

A tragic collision of two B-17s, photographed a split second after impact.

shielded their eyes from the glare of the early morning sun. Looking up they could see that two tiny silver bombers were locked together nearly three miles above them, and then the aircraft appeared to break up. "Bloody Hell" said Alf, and he ran off to get help. An oily black smudge appeared in the sky, surrounded by hundreds of flashing and sparkling pieces. Just below this smudge another B-17 could be seen spiralling around, minus one of its wings. The results of the collision had been seen by people as far away as Letchworth and Stevenage, some people even began to cheer, believing that the aircraft were German.

Hearing the sound of the explosion a three year old boy looked up, then

ran indoors. Grabbing at his mother's apron strings in child-like innocence he said, "Mummy, mummy there's something wrong in the sky."

The weather so far indicated that this would be a glorious summer's day. The runways of Parham airfield already shimmered in the early morning heat and, as the crews gathered, a lone skylark trilled high above them. Each aeroplane was standing on its dispersal point, fully fuelled and bombed up, primed for readiness. Some aircraft were still having last minute ground crew checks, emphasized by the occasional clang of dropped spanners onto the concrete.

The concrete surfaces of the runways and dispersal points had that hot stone smell about them and as each crew member clambered aboard their

The nose section of B-17 'Ding Dong Daddy'.

bomber they were met with the heady odour of hot leather, oil and paint. The mission for today was considered to be a bit of 'Milk Run' instead of a long deep penetration raid it was only to the Brest Peninsular. The targets were German heavy artillery guns that had been shelling the Brest region, and holding up the Allied capture of the port.

The first Wright-Cyclone engines spluttered to life and the base reverberated with a growing vibrating roar that carried for miles around the surrounding countryside. By 7.33am the 390th`s aeroplanes were all airborne, engines straining with the weight of fuel and bomb loads. Now began the long task of waiting for all the other participating groups, in order to stack up over East Anglia.

The cloud was quite thin on this day and from high above the crews could see the patchwork quilt of the English countryside. Looking around they began to see other formations, indeed the sky looked full. Some crews were watching the lead ship in the formation B-17 42-102936. Suddenly this aircraft appeared to fly too close under the Lead Squadron. This action forced the No.4 position B-17 right into the prop wash of the lead element of three B-17s.

B-17 42-97182 was violently swung about by the prop wash and forced downwards towards B-17 42-102936. Crews watched, but the event was nothing unusual in such congested skies. Many crews from other B-17s were later to state they were uncertain as to whether 182 had come down on 936, or 936 had risen up too steeply below 182. However, the two aircraft began to get perilously close, "936 will you please let down a little" crackled over the intercoms.

A split second after this the two B-17s locked together. 182's propeller blades slashed into the vertical stabiliser of 936, throwing small shreds of metal everywhere. Larger fragments of 936's stabiliser and fuselage began to be torn away. Frederick Walsh, the top turret gunner on board 936, remembered looking up and seeing the propeller tips from 182 cutting off the barrels of his 0.50 calibre machine guns. 936's wing surfaces began to disintegrate and fall away; both aircraft tumbled over to the right-hand side and went down in a sheet of white flame.

A short while afterwards the bombs aboard 936 began to detonate in the air and then the bomber simply exploded in a brilliant white flash. The navigator, Raymond Klausing, was immediately blown clean through the Plexiglas nose cone; miraculously he came to his senses, pulled his ripcord, and lived to tell his story.

All that was left of 936 was a huge dark oily pall of smoke and loads of downwards spiralling debris.

A B-17 of the 390th Bomb Group at Parham, similar to the two bombers that collided over Weston.

Many of 936's crew had been blown from their aircraft and, like Raymond Klausing, had managed to deploy their chutes. However exploding bombs created shock waves that sucked them back towards and into the descending fireball. Other parachute canopies caught alight and accompanying crews watched in horror as the bodies of their colleagues and friends fell to earth. Of the nine men in this crew only four would survive. Having exploded with such violence, 936 now consisted of several large sections tumbling to earth.

These included the cockpit/forward fuselage section and one wing. The other wing with engines still screaming was spiralling down, leaving a long trail of flame and smoke. The tail section floated down with what was left of the

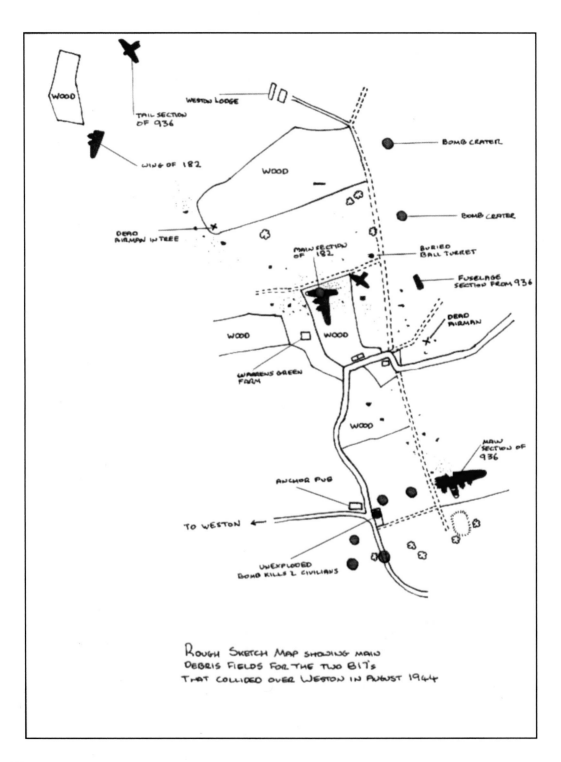

WOOD

WESTON LODGE

TAIL SECTION OF 936

WING OF 182

WOOD

BOMB CRATER

BOMB CRATER

DEAD AIRMAN IN TREE

MAIN SECTION OF 182

BURIED BALL TURRET

FUSELAGE SECTION FROM 936

DEAD AIRMAN

WOOD

WOOD

WARRENS GREEN FARM

WOOD

MAIN SECTION OF 936

ANCHOR PUB

TO WESTON

UNEXPLODED BOMB KILLS 2 CIVILIANS

ROUGH SKETCH MAP SHOWING MAIN DEBRIS FIELDS FOR THE TWO BITS THAT COLLIDED OVER WESTON IN AUGUST 1944 rear fuselage. The forward fuselage and cockpit section was full of flames and Frederick Walsh, dazed and semi-conscious, was trapped by the huge centrifugal forces. He managed to grab a parachute pack that was stuck on a piece of jagged metal. Finally clipping it on he was able to jump clear, but was badly burned.

The pilot and co-pilot of 936, either trapped or overcome by flames, remained in the nose section of the aircraft as it fell. It floated down and impacted just behind Friends Green Cottages, where it erupted into a huge fireball, shortly followed by the sound of exploding ammunition.

One eyewitness, Eric Buckle, recalled seeing the burned and crumpled cockpit containing two charred bodies. Trapped in 936's rear fuselage section as it tumbled through the sky were Lotus Conser, Robert Hunter and Richard McAteer. After baling out McAteer briefly glimpsed Hunter and Conser up front, both also about to get out, but Hunter could not locate his parachute and desperately grabbed Conser so that they could bail out together. When Conser pulled his rip cord the canopy opened fast due to their combined weight and the jolt loosened the slightly dazed Hunter's grip. Despite frantic efforts Robert Hunter continued to slide down Conser's body. He began to lose his hold until he was hanging onto both of Conser's flying boots, then only one, then he was gone. Lotus Conser looked away as the young man started a fall of over 10,000 feet that would terminate in a small meadow by Warrens Green. His body left an imprint in the field which was still visible in the early 1950s.

Of the survivors, Raymond Klausing landed in the vicinity of Fairclough Hall, Richard McAteer came down close to Lotus Conser in the grounds of Weston Lodge. The rear fuselage section they had managed to escape from slammed to earth in a field some quarter-of-a-mile away. Frederick Walsh landed nearly a mile away from these three in a field near the Anchor Pub.

At this time wreckage from 936 was still coming to earth over a wide area. Larger parts of 936's structure had hit the ground around the same time as the one-winged 182 had fallen into the wood. One large part fell at Halls Green and set fire to a hayrick. 936's engines broke away in the air and smashed to ground nearby, one actually hitting

The tail section from B-17 42-102936 at Halls Green.

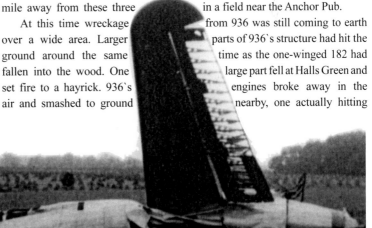

Warrens Green farmhouse. Inside were John Buckle, his wife and young son, all luckily unharmed. Upon walking around their house to look at the damage an awful sight greeted them; there on the lawn was a severed hand.

Also nearby the smashed remains of a pearl handled Smith & Wesson revolver were found. Numerous bombs now began to explode as they hit the ground. Tragically one bomb that did not explode punched straight through the roof of a small bungalow, splintering a huge beam. Inside the bungalow a wartime evacuee, Mrs Webb, had been bathing a small child David Clements, both were killed.

As more bombs began exploding across the fields from the Anchor Pub a young boy John Clements (brother of David) was seriously injured by a large lump of clay. Next door to the Clements family lived Charles Grass, who also had witnessed the collision high above. He ran for cover with his wife towards a nearby ditch as bombs began bursting all around them. Mrs Grass was thrown to the ground by an explosion just 30 yards away.

As they sheltered they noticed an American airman drifting down towards them, Frederick Walsh, who landed and appeared to be shouting at them to take cover. Charles Grass did not heed any such warnings and bravely ran over to assist the airman. Mr and Mrs Pearce from the Anchor Pub also ran out to help. As Charles Grass got to the young airmen he heard the words, "I'm burning up, please take this gum outta my mouth." Getting Frederick Walsh out of his harness was no easy task, but the rescuers managed to release him and get him to the ditch. Frederick Walsh would later join the Irving founded Caterpillar Club and Charles Grass went on to receive a Civil Award for his bravery that day.

The crumpled tail section of Ding Dong Daddy. It is still possible to find small parts of the bomber in the plough soil here.

Another crewman from 936 who had managed to bale out safely was gathering up his parachute when a jagged piece of airframe fell from the sky, piercing his chest and killing him. So far the identity of this crew member has not been ascertained, but surely he must rank as one of the unluckiest individuals from any air crash in this period.

Within a short time a USAAF fire tender arrived along with several local appliances. Another eye-witness was Robert Rand, who despite only being ten years old had been brought to the scene in a jeep from nearby Nuthampstead. He remembers arriving at the scene and several people turning over a large section of fuselage only to find a body stuck underneath. A doctor from Baldock by the name of Renton-Riddle was called to the scene to administer medication to survivors. Some hours later, his job done, he stopped outside the Anchor Pub. There on the grass verge lay an unexploded bomb and bloodstained kit bags full of human remains.

Meanwhile the other B-17, 182, had begun its slow descent to earth some minutes before. One of its wings broke away and the ball turret 'popped out' of the fuselage section as it buckled. Now totally un-aerodynamic and spiralling, other bomber crews could see the sunlight reflecting from 182's Plexiglas fittings and falling debris, as could people on the ground far below. A wing fluttered earthwards with engines under full power, after several minutes this wing hit the ground in a sheet of flame beside a small wood near Halls Green.

Having plummeted thousands of feet, no one had yet managed to bale out from 182. The centrifugal forces probably made escape impossible. One can but imagine the terror and fear of those young men trapped inside their burning and

The old 'Anchor Pub' in 2007 and now a house. The dead crewmen and several bombs were placed on the grass verge, approximately where the large stones now lie.

disintegrating bomber for what must have seemed an eternity.

Finally, as the bomber levelled out into a flat spin, the tail unit broke away just before it fell into the end of a small wood at Warrens Green and ended the suffering. A huge fireball rose up, ammunition began to explode and then a single bomb that had been stuck in the bomb-bay detonated, scattering twigs, branches and lumps of clay over a wide area. The force of this blast also scattered pieces of 182 and her crew throughout the wood. The blast also damaged the roof of a nearby cottage and surrounding trees had large branches torn away. Much of this small wood was now ablaze as were several cornfields in the vicinity.

The rest of the B-17s undertook their raid and landed back at Parham. The German guns had been destroyed totally, the only defence being some very light flak. On Sunday 27 August the local Home Guard began the job of scouring Weston Park, looking for unexploded ordnance and body parts from 182.

On the far right of this photo is Sgt Richard A McAteer who was the Tail Gunner on B-17 42-102936, of the 18 men involved in the collision he was one of only four to survive. (Courtesy of M and J Huffman)

However, it was summertime and dense undergrowth prevented them finding very much. Frank Hawkes and some friends were out looking for 'souvenirs' when one of them spotted a parachute canopy billowing out from the top of a tall conifer. One of them then climbed up to get this precious item, but perhaps it wasn't the best idea as wrapped up inside it and pinned to the tree was a dead airman. The lads pelted off to find the local policeman and on their way to the village found a flying boot still with the foot inside.

The remains of 182's crew were still being gathered from Warrens Spring wood for weeks afterwards, many locals say that the woodland smelt of burnt wood, oil, rubber and flesh for ages. One ex-poacher told me it was pointless taking ferrets into the wood to look for rabbits, as they were distracted by the shreds of decaying flesh everywhere.

Another local man, Tom Clements, thought he had made a really interesting keepsake. He spotted an American service issue cap lying in a bed of nettles, thinking it was a shame the brass badge was missing he turned it over and dropped it quickly…a large section of hair and skull was stuck inside it.

When the ball turret had broken away from 182`s fuselage high above Weston Park that day Michael Kasarda, the gunner, was trapped inside it. Eventually both the spherical turret and his body rammed some six feet deep into the chalky clay of a field near Weston Lodge. The turret and its contents were discovered only when someone went to investigate the hole to see if it contained an unexploded bomb, and noticed two 0.50 gun barrels poking upwards from the bottom.

When they had recovered, Frank Hawkes and his friends decided to go and see some large sections of 936 that had come to the ground near Dane End. Inside the fuselage they noticed it was awash with blue dinghy dye and many sealed drinking water tins lay about. Some of the Plexiglas from both aircraft was later fashioned into jewellery and at least one parachute went on to become lingerie for local ladies. One local man went to the site some days later and found a petrol cigarette lighter; amazingly he still has it today, and its still works!

182's wing at Halls Green stayed for many years, sunlight and the elements slowly fading its bright blue star and bar insignia, until one day it was moved and hung up in a barn to shield farm implements from bird droppings. It survived until the 1970s then, like so many artefacts of this nature, it was sold to a passing scrap dealer; an ignominious ending for such a tragic relic.Souveniring was not always for personal gain, more often to obtain and acquire a memento from a traumatic incident. Some locals, however, were looking for personal gain from the tragedy, like those who drained fuel from a ruptured fuel tank to power private vehicles. The fuel was found to be far too rich, but not before several cars' engine cylinders had been burned out.

Also within this mass of wreckage one lad found a dinghy, which he later hid. He was caught by a local policeman using this whilst right in the middle of a lake and was given a severe ticking off.

The author's son Bertie points to where the main part of B-17, 42-102936 crashed.

One young man living in Graveley was on leave from the Army when the collision occurred. "Walking across the fields to Weston. I came to the crash site. Looking around I spotted a 0.50 Browning machine gun with some linked bullets. Stupidly I bent down and pressed the trigger, sending a stream of bullets very close to some local boys who were playing around the area. As a tank gunner I was only too aware of how stupid my actions were."

Of the four aircrew from 936 who survived the collision Raymond Klausing, Frederick Walsh and Richard McAteer sadly all passed away in 1998 leaving just one, Lotus Conser.

SINCE 1944

The woodland was cleared a few months after the collision; however a few mature trees still bearing evidence of the crash of 182 were left. In the 1970s Den Mathews, a ploughman, was in a field near Weston Lodge when his plough snagged a large item, almost stalling his tractor. Upon removal it was seen to be a Browning 0.50 machine gun, one almost certainly originating from B-17 936.

In the 1970s it was still possible to see quite large sections of 182 in the wood where she came down, such as a huge section of rubberised self sealing fuel tank, several trees also had debris sticking out from their trunks and branches. Numerous individuals have searched the wood and removed items over the years. Recently a Lieutenant's cap badge was found in two battered pieces, parts of the throttle quadrants, instruments and sections of control column from 182 have all been found in the wood.

In 2002 the wood was again cleared, this time many mature trees were not so lucky, now only three trees show scars and breakages attributable to when B-17 182 smashed into them. New undergrowth is sprouting quickly, hiding the blue powdery patches that show where another piece of metal is slowly oxidising in the damp soil.

The exact spot today where the crumpled tail section of 'Ding Dong Daddy' lay in 1944 (compare with picture on page 110).

In 2005 the tip of one of the control column yokes of B-17 182 was found, sticking out from a patch of disturbed soil at the edge of the wood.

At the end of a summer's day when there is a good sunset it is still possible to see shadows across the fields from long ago filled in bomb craters. The cottage that had its roof damaged now has a large extension hiding the repairs. The cottage where Mrs Webb and John Clements were killed still exists, and if one looks carefully repair to roof tiles and brickwork can just be made out.

One of the largest reminders is in Warrens Spring wood, where 182 crashed, for here the single bomb that detonated has left a large crater that still exists today. It is difficult to imagine the loss of life and violence that happened in this small wood. These days the only real noise and disturbance in this wood emanates from the rather aggressive pair of Moorhens that nest each year on the dark earthy water filled bomb crater.

Note: - During the compilation of this book the author received an e-mail from Mr M.Huffmann, who lives in the United States, his wife Janet is the daughter of Richard McAteer

Lt Robert G. Taylor the navigator on board the B-17 named 'Ding Dong Daddy' he was killed along with the rest of his crew as a result of the collision. He was aged just 21 years.

(Courtesy Mark Bettinson and other members of Robert Taylor's family)

the tail gunner from B-17 42-102936. Shortly before he died in 1998 Richard McAteer wrote a brief account of what had happened fifty four years before and it is a privilege to be able to quote an excerpt from that account in his own words.

"I heard on the intercom Sgt Walsh call the pilot to drop the aircraft as there was an aircraft coming down on top of us. I looked up from my tail position and looked right into the tail wheel-well of the aircraft coming down on us. Then there was a crash and explosion. The craft above was just far enough back that his propellers chewed into our right wing. There was an explosion, when smoke cleared I was in the waist section that had blown off. I crawled forward to the waist door and saw Conser and Hunter in the end of the waist preparing to jump. I salvoed the door and went out."

Just before this book went to press another relative, this time one of the crew of 'Ding Dong Daddy' made contact with the author. This was Mark Bettinson who is the nephew of Robert Taylor, the navigator. Mark has in his possession letters, photographs and artefacts relating to the flying career of Robert Taylor and most of his crew colleagues. He forwarded some of the photographs to me, allowing me, for the first time in over three decades of research, to finally see the faces of the men whose names had become so familiar.

'THE PEACEMAKER' INCIDENT.

Aircraft:	Crew:
B-17G Flying Fortress Serial Number 43-37552	Pilot. 2nd Lt Hollis Forbes… Killed
401 Squadron, 91st Bombardment Group	Co-Pilot. 2nd Lt Henry P Maximovich…Killed
(Heavy)	Radio Operator. Sgt Albert L Johnston…Killed
Based at Bassingbourn in Cambridgeshire	Top Turret Gunner. S/Sgt Harold E Good…Killed
Location:	Crew Chief. M/Sgt Lester B Culp…Killed
In large field adjacent to Weston Park.	Passenger. Major John C Walker…Killed
Time:	
15.45 hours	

On 12 April 1945 a B-17 Flying Fortress took off from Bassingbourn for a routine slow engine timing flight. At 15.45 hours an unknown aircraft radioed back to the base that a B-17 had crashed at Weston. Lieutenant Niller was flying another B-17 near the base and was requested to have a look and confirm the report. He reported that there was indeed a B-17 down in Weston Park and all he could see on the tail fin were the numbers 552. What had caused the B-17 to come down during what should have been a routine flight?

At least one eye-witness reports that the aircraft passed over Weston several times and on the last pass one engine seemed to be on fire. Unfortunately this cannot be confirmed and, since there were no eyewitnesses to the actual impact, the reasons for the crash remain a mystery to this day.

The Peacemaker at Bassingbourn. This shot clearly shows the emotive nose-art design.

Several eye witnesses do state that whilst circling the village the bomber seemed to bank and come over extremely low. Were the crew attempting to impress their passenger?

On board was Major John C Walker, who had only asked to join the flight at the last minute …. he just fancied a local flight. Was it a flock of birds causing a bird strike, or had the crew spotted some pretty Land Army girls below and were trying to show off? We cannot be sure.

'The Peacemaker' had been in the air for about two hours, conducting wide circuits over the north Hertfordshire countryside. The huge Wright-Cyclone engines roared as the Boeing came in really low over a field, unusually brown in appearance, having been ploughed just the day before.

As the silver bomber approached a slight valley a large flock of sea gulls and wood pigeons arose from the field, disturbed by the noise. The flock of birds scattered in all directions about 200 yards in front of the B-17. The pilot, Hollis Forbes, had to take violent evasive action and swung his huge bomber to the right-hand side of the valley. He now not only had to avoid the birds, but a tall belt of mature Elm trees that loomed rapidly into sight.

Tragically it was too little too late. The right wing tip slightly scuffed the freshly ploughed surface and, at some 150mph, the wing tip began to dig into the soft soil. The navigation light splintered and the smooth surfaced aluminium skinning began to buckle, then the wing tip folded, collapsed and broke away.

The heavier wing stub began to create an ever deepening furrow in the soil, pulling the bomber over, then the first engine hit the soil. This cart-wheeled the entire B-17 over. The propeller blades sliced into the flint ridden soil before bending and finally ceasing to rotate. The second, third and fourth engines smashed to the ground. The nose section with all on board was catapulted against the ground and smashed into the third engine with its wildly rotating propeller. As the fuselage tried to continue the cart-wheeling motion, extreme forces snapped off the tail section and flung it over 70 yards until it came to rest by a small hedge. While all this was happening the fuel tanks ruptured and exploded, sending up a huge billowing ball of flame, capped with thick black smoke.

As the choking smoke began to drift towards Weston the locals realised that for the third time in eight months an aircraft had crashed on the outskirts of their village.

The massive engines had made four deep holes in the surface of the field and around these debris was littered for over 100 yards. From within the blaze came the pop and crack of exploding ammunition and the occasional coloured flare fizzed wildly, shooting across the field.

The shattered cockpit lay in the vicinity of the third engine, whose twisted and contorted propeller blades were becoming blackened in the blaze.

Local lad Frank Hawkes ran up the lane and into the field, stopping to look at the huge tail-plane against the hedge. "I remember seeing the plastic tube from out of which the tail gunner could have a pee sticking out from the dented tail turret section," he later said. He then ran back to the village. Later, when the crash site was cleared, Frank went back to have a look. Careful searching in a nearby ditch revealed a steel flak helmet and the pink coloured ID booklet belonging to Major Walker. Frank had these for many years until, when he was on National Service in the fifties, his mother decided to spring clean the house and consign these treasures to the dust bin.

61 YEARS ON

Even today the field where 'The Peacemaker' crashed has areas of heat fractured flints, burned clay and huge areas of aluminium fragments with exploded 0.50 shell cases. Not all of the items were recovered at the time, either by the crash recovery team or indeed the many eager schoolboys who scoured the site.

In 2004 two burned and twisted three-penny coins dated 1943 were found there. For nearly sixty years the dog tag of Lester Culp had been slowly moved around the site by the plough. That is until a local metal detectorist had a signal and finally removed the tag from a clump of sticky clay one wet December afternoon in 2000.

The family of Lester Culp were traced and the dog tag returned to them in the United States.

Recently a bunch of keys with three old pennies attached has been found on the site, there is an aluminium disc attached with the name Lt Ross on it. However, Lieutenant Ross was not a crew member, so it has been assumed that he was part of the crash recovery team.

Lester Culp's family was traced and his dog tag returned to them in the United States.

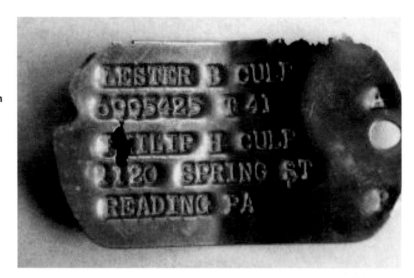

Two three penny coins found in area where the Peacemaker's cockpit fell to earth.

LIST OF HERTFORDSHIRE AVIATION CRASHES
1912-1945

Whilst every effort has been made to provide an exhaustive list, there may be some non-operational crashes that are not on record. Please note the compilers have included incidents where records are very scant or cannot be located, but in all cases evidence that the specified type of aircraft crashed (perhaps initially only based on an eyewitness account) at the location has been substantiated. Anyone with additional information is invited to contact the author via the publishers or by e-mail at Julian@redkitebooks.com

1912

6th Sept	Deperdussin of the Royal Flying Corps suffered structural failure and crashed at Graveley nr Little Wymondley – 2 killed.		

1916

3rd Sept	Schutte-Lanz AirshipSL 11 of the German Army, shot down at Cuffley – 16 Killed.		
2nd Oct	Zeppelin L31 of the German Navy, shot down at Potters Bar – 19 Killed.		

1920

July	DH 14A	G-EAPY	crashed at Hertford

1927

Sept	DH 60	G-EBRY	crashed atBushey

1929

May	DH 60X	G-EBUW	crashed at Letchworth
Oct	DH 60X	G-EBVK	crashed at Broxbourne

1931

Jan	Blackburn Bluebird 1V	G-AAOH	crashed at Bushey Park
June	Blackburn Bluebird 1V	G-AABF	crashed at Hatfield aerodrome
Dec	DH 60	G-EBOT	crashed at Broxbourne

1933

Dec	DH 82	G-ACJA	crashed atHatfield aerodrome

1934

Mar	DH 60	G-EBWT	crashed at Broxbourne

1939

	Hawker Hurricane	serial unknown	dived vertically into ground adjacent to Steeple Morden Church – pilot killed.
	Bristol Bulldog	serial unknown	smashed into trees at Weston Park – pilot killed.
26th Jan	Gloster Gladiator	serial unknown	crashed in bad weather at Baldock
13th Oct	Bristol Blenhein	L1147	crashed at Harpenden

1940

31st Jan	Bristol Blenheim 1	L6614	flew into high ground in bad weather at Royston – 2 Killed
18th Feb	Hawker Hurricane 1	L1724	dived vertically into ground at Waltham Abbey pilot killed
26th Apr	Hawker Hurricane 1	L1668	pilot baled out – crashed at Rickmansworth

25th July	Airspeed Oxford	N4757 (14 FTS)	crashed at Chipperfield
30th Aug	Messerschmitt Bf 110C-4	M8+MM	shot down at Claggybottom near Kimpton 1 killed 1 severely injured,
30th Aug	Heinkel He 111H-2	A1+CR	shot down at Hunsdon aerodrome 1 Killed 3 Injured (1 died later)
19th Sept	Heinkel He 111P	G1+GL	crashed at Thorley Wash 3 Killed 1 Injured
3rd Oct	Junkers 88A-1	3Z+BB	shot down byLight AA fire over Hatfield no injuries, crashed at East End Green
8th Oct	Hawker Hurricane	V6820 (229 Sqn)	crashed at Bovingdon – pilot killed
16th Oct	Junkers Ju 88A-5	4D+DM	crashed at Bishop's Stortford – 4 killed
17th Oct	Hawker Hurricane	V6604	force landed, no injuries at Colliers End
24th Oct	DH Tiger Moth	N6964 (24 Sqn)	hit HT cables, Borehamwood
24th Oct	DH Tiger Moth	N9327 (1 EFTS)	hit trees, Welwyn Garden City
27th Oct	Westland Lysander	P9070	undershot runway, Sawbridgeworth Airfield
18th Nov	Airspeed Oxford	P1830 (14 FTS)	crashed at Hemel Hempstead
23rd Nov	Avro Anson	R3436 (24 Sqn)	crashed at Barnet
24th Nov	Hawker Hurricane	V6916 (46 Sqn)	crashed at Bishop's Stortford
Date unconfirmed	DH Tiger Moth		crashed outside Bacon Factory in Letchworth pilot killed
Date unconfirmed	Hawker Hurricane		crash landed out of fuel, Sish Lane in Stevenage

1941

Jan	Vickers Wellington	T2550	crashed at Stapleford
16th Feb	Junkers Ju 88	V4+GS	disorientated and crash landed with no injuries, Steeple Morden aerodrome
25th Feb	Vickers Wellington 1	L4276 (11 OTU)	Stalled and spun into ground at Newnham 5 killed
28th Feb	Westland Lysander	N1217 (268 Sqn)	crashed at Rickmansworth
4th Apr	Miles Magister	N3799 (24 EFTS)	hit wires when low flying, Sandridge
9th Apr	Junkers Ju 88 A-1	F1+CC	crashed at St Pauls Walden, 4 injured
8th Apr	Heinkel He 111 H-4	1H+ET	crashed at Bendish, 1 killed 4 injured
30th Apr	Hawker Hurricane I	P3864 (52 MU)	dived vertically into ground, Bishop's Stortford pilot killed
31st May	Douglas Havoc I	BJ495	lost control in bad weather, Bishop's Stortford
21st June	Westland Lysander	R9020	stalled on landing at Sawbridgeworth airfield
24th June	DH Tiger Moth	N6863 (1 EFTS)	pilot baled out over London Colney
22nd July	Junkers Ju 88 C-4	R4+BL	Aerial collision, 3 killed, Ashwell
22nd July	Vickers Wellington IC	R1334 (11 OTU)	collision with Junkers 88 C-4 *above*. 8 killed
31st July	Supermarine Spitfire II	P2425	Loss of control after steep dive, Albury no injury to pilot
21st Aug	Douglas Boston II	AH523	Overshot runway upon landing, Hunsdon

9th Sept	Curtiss P-40 Tomahawk	AH945	undercarriage collapsed upon landing Sawbridgeworth airfield
10th Sept	Curtiss P-40 Tomahawk	AH928	undercarriage collapsed upon landing Sawbridgeworth airfield
11th Sept	Curtiss P-40 Tomahawk	AH927	undercarriage collapsed upon landing Sawbridgeworth airfield
14th Sept	Vickers Wellington	R1012 (11 OTU)	crashed at Hunsdon
5th Oct	Supermarine Spitfire	R7033 (1 PRU)	pilot thrown out of aeroplane during severe turbulence. Butlers Hall, Sawbridgeworth
22th Oct	Douglas Havoc I	AX912	spun into ground making a single engined approach. Details unconfirmed, Hunsdon
6th Nov	Supermarine Spitfire	N3161 (61 OTU)	crashed at Hemel Hempstead
19th Nov	Miles Magister I	N3952	force landed, no injuries, Ormstead Hall
21st Nov	Douglas Boston II	AH432	hit trees on circuit flight, Gilston Park
21st Nov	Supermarine Spitfire	P9439 (61 OTU)	attempted forced landing, Stevenage pilot injured
25th Nov	Hawker Hurricane I	V6916	force landed, no injuries, Bishop's Stortford
12th Dec	Hawker Hurricane IIc	BD943	dived vertically into ground near Eastwick pilot killed
16th Dec	Douglas Boston II	AH473	engine failure on approach, Hunsdon aerodrome
Date unconfirmed	DH Tiger Moth		dived vertically into field near Letchworth Gate pilot killed
Date unconfirmed	Airspeed Oxford		crash landed in field next to Letchworth Gate
Date unconfirmed	Airspeed Oxford		crash landed near Box Wood Stevenage
Date unconfirmed	Bristol Blenheim		crash landed, Bennington estate
1942			
24th Feb	Douglas Boston III	W8335	flew into high ground in bad weather 4 killed, South Bartley
29th Mar	DH Mosquito II	DD621	engine failure, Hatfield aerodrome
9th Apr	Douglas Boston II	AH476	pilot lost control whilst descending through cloud. 2 Killed, Bury Green
18th Apr	Douglas Boston III	W8276	dived vertically into ground, 3 killed, Wadford
9th May	P-51 Mustang	AG401	tipped up on landing
9th May	P-51 Mustang	AG403	collided upon landing with aircraft below
9th May	P-51 Mustang	AG488	collided upon landing with aircraft above
26th May	Supermarine Spitfire V	W3714	overshot runway in bad weather Hatfield aerodrome
June	Hawker Hotspur	BT605	crashed at Weston
10th June	DH Mosquito FII	DD603	aircraft broke up during night flying training 2 killed, Stansted Mountfitchett
28th June	Vickers Wellington	R1445 (11 OTU)	possibly shot down by nightfighter. 2 killed, crashed onto house in Ashwell
29th June	Vickers Wellington	X3173 (11 OTU)	crashed at Ashwell, 3 killed 2 Injured

1st Aug	Douglas Boston II	AH475	engine failure, Hunsdon
30th Aug	Douglas Havoc II	AH452	starboard engine failure, 2 killed, Hunsdon
23rd Sept	Curtiss P-40E	41-36028 (92 BG)	crashed Berkhampstead railway station pilot killed
29th Oct	P-51 Mustang I	AG605	flew into high ground in bad weather, Ware pilot killed
29th Oct	P-51 Mustang 1	AG633	crashed in bad weather, Sawbridgeworth
23rd Nov	DH Mosquito		collision with a/c below. 2 injured. Near Brent Pelham
23rd Nov	DH Mosquito		collision with a/c above. 2 killed. Near Nazeing
23rd Nov	B-17 Flying Fortress	DF-G 41-24506 (91 BG)	Hit pylon attempting to land at Leavesden, 5 killed 5 safe
25th Nov	P-40 Tomahawk IIB	AK144	dived vertically into ground, Sawbridgeworth pilot killed
28th Nov	DH Mosquito II	DD741	crash landed after engine failure, Hunsdon 1 killed
6th Dec	Miles Magister I	ATA	dived into ground, Letchworth, pilot killed
Date unconfirmed	Supermarine Spitfire		crashed near Baldock Radio Station, pilot killed

1943

2nd Feb	Supermarine Spitfire IX		crashed near Elstree High Street, pilot killed
3rd Feb	Vickers Wellington	N2906 (24 Sqn)	crashed at Dosetts Farm
16th Feb	Hawker Typhoon Ic	DN422	aborted take-off and flew into crash tender Sawbridgeworth airfield
26th Feb	Short Stirling	BF445	overshot Stansted on two engines crashed at Thremhall Priory nr Bishop's Stortford
23rd Mar	Auster	MZ139	crashed trying to avoid pursuing Mosquito 1 injured. Near Little Hormead
23rd Mar	Auster	MZ161	crashed trying to avoid pursuing Mosquito 1 injured. Near Furneaux Pelham
3rd Apr	P-47c Thunderbolt		caught fire and crashed on approach to runway pilot killed. Sawbridgeworth airfield
June	Supermarine Spitfire	AB503	details unconfirmed – Sawbridgeworth
5th July	P-51 Mustang I	AP220	crashed whilst rolling at low altitude pilot killed. Sawbridgeworth
23rd Aug	DH Mosquito VI	HX849	broke up in mid-air after collision 2 killed, St Albans
23rd Aug	DH Mosquito VI	HX850	collision with above aircraft, 2 killed, St Albans
27th Aug	P-47C Thunderbolt	41-6365 (78 FG)	spun in and crashed at Bennington House, 6 miles ESE of Stevenage, pilot killed
31st Aug	DH Mosquito II	DZ379	stalled after high speed turn, 2 killed, crashed at Stansted Abbotts
3rd Sept	AW Whitley V	AD679	flew into ground during night flying practice Finch Lane at Bushey
14th Sept	Supermarine Spitfire IX	MA754	crash landed, pilot killed, Rickmansworth

29th Sept	P-47D Thunderbolt	HL-P	forced landing, no injuries, Nuthampstead
20th Oct	AW Whitley V	BD280 (10 OTU)	stalled avoiding high tension cables, Evinghoe
22nd Oct	Avro Lancaster Mk I	L7575	broke up in mid-air, 7 Killed, over Colney Heath
24th Nov	P-51 Mustang IA	FD483 (170 Sqn)	crashed half a mile South of Whitehall, pilot killed
2nd Dec	P-38H Lightning	CY-M (55 FG)	engine failure edge of Nuthampstead, pilot safe
3rd Dec	Vickers Wellington IA	N2906	severe crash landing, 4 killed, Dossetts Farm
11th Dec	P-38H Lightning	KI-Z 42-67052 (20 FG)	landing accident Nuthampstead, pilot safe
31st Dec	B-17G Flying Fortress	GY-N 42-31327 (306 BG)	ran out of fuel returning from raid on Bordeaux / Merignac. 1 seriously injured 7 minor injuries. Hit a tree at Walkern
31st Dec	B-17G Flying Fortress	YB-M 42-37774 (351 BG)	ran out of fuel returning from raid on Bordeaux / Merignac. Crew baled out safely, Horn Hill at Preston
31st Dec	B-17G Flying Fortress 'Fool's Luck'	SC-D 42-31068 (401 BG)	abandoned returning in bad weather from raid on Bordeaux / Merignac, Foxhole Hill, Potters Bar
31st Dec	B-17G Flying Fortress	SC-D 42-31528 (305 BG)	abandoned returning in bad weather from Bordeaux / Merignac, Ashridge 4 killed 6 safe

1944

4th Jan	Short Stirling	N3675 (1657 CU)	Hunsdon	
10th Jan	P-38J Lightning		landing accident, Nuthampstead	
23rd Jan	DH Mosquito VI	HJ774	stalled in slipstream of another aircraft 2 killed, 1 Mile south of Hunsdon	
2nd Feb	P-47C Thunderbolt	VF-E	forced Landing	Nuthampstead
2nd Feb	P-47D Thunderbolt	VF-H	forced Landing	Nuthampstead
2nd Feb	P-47D Thunderbolt	VF-K	forced Landing	Nuthampstead
2nd Feb	P-47C Thunderbolt	VF-D	forced Landing	Nuthampstead
11th Feb	P-47D Thunderbolt	HL-T	crash Landing, Great Hormead, pilot killed	
24th Feb	DH Mosquito FB.VI	RNZAF	crashed on take off, 2 killed, Nuthampstead	
27th Feb	DH Mosquito III		crashed on take off, Nuthampstead	
3rd Mar	HP Halifax B III	LW516	port inner engine failed, aircraft then broke up over Hexton, 1 killed	
3rd Mar	DH Mosquito XVI	MM337	landing accident, Nuthampstead	
10th Mar	DH Mosquito VI	HX809	hit balloon cable, no injuries, Buntingford	
16th Mar	P-51B Mustang	OS-S	belly Landed, Royston	
24th Mar	B-17G Flying Fortress	JD-Z	crash Landed, 2 miles west of Nuthampstead	
31st Mar	Avro Lancaster Mk II	LL683	ran out of fuel after raid on Nurnberg no injuries, Sawbridgeworth	
1st July	DH Mosquito XIII	MM516	stalled, 2 killed, Bishop's Stortford	
18th July	Avro Lancaster Mk III	LM616	sustained AA damage during raid on Emieville 7 killed, Great Offley	
24th July	Avro Lancaster Mk III	JB417	emergency landing, caught fire,1 injured, Radlett	

31st July	Douglas A-20G		crash landed, Little Hadham
5th Aug	DH Mosquito VI	HP848	struck trees whilst flying too low, 2 killed, Colliers End
9th Aug	DH Mosquito XIII	HK406	starboard engine broke away, 2 killed, Hunsdon
11th Aug	P-51B Mustang	D7-Y	forced landing, Nuthampstead
12th Aug	B-24 Liberator	DC-Y+	aerial collision, 9 killed, Cheshunt
12th Aug	B-17G Flying Fortress	42-107191	aerial Collision with above aircraft, 9 killed, Lude Farm at Loudwater
26th Aug	B-17G Flying Fortress	42-97182	aerial collision, 5 killed 4 injured, Weston Park
26th Aug	B-17G Flying Fortress	42-102936	aerial collision with above aircraft 9 killed, Weston Park
30th Aug	B-26B Marauder	42-95953	severe crash, Standon
15th Octr	B-17G Flying Fortress	42-97746	crashed on take off, 10 killed, Anstey Church
1st Nov	DH Mosquito VI	MS850	engine cut out, overshot runway, caught fire, no injuries, Hunsdon aerodrome
14th Nov	Hawker Tempest V	EJ551	engine cut out, no injuries, 1 mile east of Standon
16th Nov	P-51D Mustang	B7-R	dived into ground, Kelshall
12th Dec	Mosquito NF30	MV342	hit by lightning strike, causing belly landing no injuries, Hunsdon aerodrome
24th Dec	B-17G Flying Fortress	42-102536	crashed on take off, 2 killed, Nuthampstead
Date unconfirmed	B-17G Flying Fortress		crash landed, Barley
Date unconfirmed	P-47 Thunderbolt		crash landed at very high speed, Bennington pilot killed

1945

1st Jan	DH Mosquito NF30	NT253	stalled on approach, 2 killed, Hunsdon
4th Jan	DH Mosquito Mk XIII	MM558	pilot landed too fast, overshot runway no injuries, Hunsdon aerodrome
19th Jan	DH Mosquito Mk XIII	MM568	on landing, drop tank hit ground and aircraft caught fire. No injuries, Hunsdon aerodrome
3rd Feb	DH Mosquito Mk XIII	HK513	pilot landed too fast, overshot runway, no injuries, Hunsdon aerodrome
6th Feb	P-51D Mustang	6N-0	crashed at Puckeridge, pilot killed
11th Feb	P-51D Mustang	QP-W	dived into ground, Barkway, pilot killed
12th Apr	B-17G Flying Fortress	43-37552	mis-timed engines causing stall / bird strike? 6 Killed, Weston Park
April	DH Mosquito	MM814	crashed near Bishop's Stortford
May	HP Halifax	NA291	crashed at Garston
11th June	P-51B Mustang	OS-(J)	dived into ground, 3 miles South of Royston

Town/Village	Total Number of times targetted	Total Number of Confirmed Bombs Landed	Total HE Bombs Confirmed as Landed	Total Inc Bombs Confirmed as Landed	Total LRR's Confirmed as Landed	Total MBB's Confirmed as Landed	Total PM's Confirmed as Landed	Total UIM's Confirmed as Landed	Total V-1's Confirmed as Landed
Albury	12	229	15	210	0	0	4	0	0
Anstey	7	32	20	12	0	0	0	0	0
Barkway	6	10	7	2	0	0	1	0	0
Barley	17	261	29	231	0	0	0	1	0
Braughing	7	49	26	22	1	0	0	0	0
Brent Pelham	7	20	15	4	0	0	1	0	0
Buckland	2	4	3	1	0	0	0	0	0
Buntingford	5	21	20	1	0	0	0	0	0
Burden	1	2	0	0	0	0	2	0	0
Chipping	1	3	3	0	0	0	0	0	0
Colliers End	3	12	10	0	0	2	0	0	0
Cottered	5	11	8	0	0	0	2	0	1
Dassells	1	1	0	0	0	0	0	0	1
Furneaux Pelham	6	5*	3	1*	1	0	0	0	0
Great Hormead	4	11	4	7	0	0	0	0	0
Great Munden	3	23	23	0	0	0	0	0	0
High Cross	4	3*	0*	3*	0	0	0	0	0
Kelshall	2	5	3	2	0	0	0	0	0
Latchford Lodge	1	2	0	0	0	0	2	0	0
Levens Green	1	1	0	1	0	0	0	0	0
Little Hadham	13	90	28	62	0	0	0	0	0
Little Hormead	2	6	5	1	0	0	0	0	0
Meesden	2	9	8	0	0	0	0	0	1
Much Hadham	10	227*	24	200*	1	0	0	0	2
Nuthampstead	3	4	3	0	1	0	0	0	0
Old Hall Green	1	1	0	0	0	0	1	0	0
Puckeridge	2	0*	0*	0*	0	0	0	0	0
Reed	3	4	3	1	0	0	0	0	0
Rush Green	1	2	2	0	0	0	0	0	0
Sandon	11	156*	53	101*	1	1	0	0	0
St. Edmunds College	1	1	0	0	0	0	1	0	0
Standon	16	233*	32*	200*	0	0	0	0	1
Stocking Pelham	4	5	3	1	0	0	1	0	0
Therfield	1	1	1	0	0	0	0	0	0